**PETRICĂ VLAD**

# AMAZON EDITION
# SILICON EMPATHY
## INSPIRING A DIGITAL UTOPIA THROUGH THE FUSION OF AI AND HUMAN CONNECTION

BUCUREȘTI, 2024

© Petrică Vlad

Copyright 2024 Digitalize-d SRL
All rights reserved

No part of this publication may be reproduced, stored in or introduced into a retrieval system, or transmitted, in any form, or by any means (electronic, mechanical, photocopying, recording, or otherwise), without the prior permission of the publisher. Requests for permission should be directed to contact@digitalize-d.com


Petrică Vlad
Bucharest, Romania
www.petricavlad.com

ISBN 9798327110618
Printed by Amazon

The web addresses referenced in this book were live and correct at the time of the book's publication but may be subject to change.

To the people that gave me life.
　To the people that gave my life meaning.
　　To the technology that touched my life.
　　　To the people that read this book.

# ABOUT THE AUTHOR

Petrică Vlad - born in Bucharest on the 17th of June, 1999, is a distinguished figure in the digital transformation and artificial intelligence sphere. His profound impact on Fortune 500 companies globally, through roles such as Regional Transformation Manager, EMEA and Global GenAI Expert at Teleperformance, has established him as a pivotal force in advancing AI technologies within the corporate world.

With academic credentials from the University of "Valahia" of Targoviste and a Master's Degree from the Bucharest University of Economic Studies, Petrica's journey is a testament to the power of education and the pursuit of excellence. His contributions have not only optimized customer experiences and streamlined business processes but also demonstrated remarkable ROI, showcasing his strategic prowess.

Petrica's influence extends beyond boardrooms and into international forums, where he has captivated audiences in Greece, Germany, and the UAE as a keynote speaker. His insights on innovation, leadership, and the technological future are both enlightening and inspiring.

Moreover, as a startup advisor, Petrica dedicates his extensive experience to nurturing emerging companies, guiding them towards sustainable growth and success. His debut book promises to encapsulate his vast knowledge and experiences, offering readers a unique perspective on navigating the complexities of the digital age.

**Prologue**

**Chapter 1: The Genesis of Silicon Empathy**
- The Dawn of Artificial Intelligence
- From Mechanical Brains to Emotional Beings
- The Inspiration Behind Silicon Empathy

**Chapter 2: Understanding AI**
- The Basics of AI: What It Is and Isn't
- Different Flavors of AI: NLP, Foundational & Generative
- How AI Is Changing the World

**Chapter 3: The Human Connection**
- The Essence of Empathy in Technology
- Stories of Technology Touching Lives
- The Gap AI Can't Fill... Yet

**Chapter 4: Silicon Empathy in Action**
- Case Studies from Industry Giants
- Small Businesses and Startups: A New Frontier
- The Role of AI in Enhancing Customer Experience

**Chapter 5: The Ethical Dimensions of AI**
- Navigating the Moral Maze
- Privacy, Security, and Trust in an AI-Driven World
- The Responsibility of Creators

**Chapter 6: Building a Bridge between AI and Humanity**
- Designing with Empathy: Principles and Practices
- Encouraging Emotional Intelligence in AI Development
- The Importance of Keeping Humans in the Loop

**Chapter 7: The Future Is Now**
- Emerging Technologies and Their Potential
- Silicon Empathy: A Vision for the Future
- The Road Ahead: Challenges and Opportunities

**Epilogue**

# PROLOGUE

Dear Reader,

As I sat down to write this book, my head was filled not with a rigid blueprint but with a conviction: the knowledge and experiences I've gathered through my journey in the fields of technology and digital transformation were not solely my own to keep. They were insights to be shared, lessons to be passed on. In 2023, I introduced the concept of Silicon Empathy at a major digital business conference. It was a term that encapsulated my belief in the symbiotic relationship between human insight and artificial intelligence, a concept that was warmly embraced by many and has since guided my work and vision.

'Silicon Empathy' is more than a buzzword; it's a pathway to a future where technology transcends its binary constraints and begins to understand the nuances of human emotion and connection. This book is an exploration of that future. It's about understanding the roots of AI, from the rudimentary algorithms of the past to the sophisticated, generative models of today that can mimic human language and creativity. But it's also about recognizing the importance of keeping our humanity in the loop, ensuring that as we advance technologically, we do not lose sight of the values and connections that define us.

Throughout this journey, we'll dive into the mechanics of AI, demystifying the complex web of foundational, generative, and natural language processing technologies. We'll explore how these tools are being used to revolutionize customer experiences across industries, making services more personalized, efficient, and, crucially, more human. From arts to customer service, AI has the potential to enhance our creativity, solve complex problems, and connect us in ways we've only begun to imagine.

Yet, as we chart this course towards a digital utopia, Silicon Empathy urges us to pause and consider: how do we ensure that this future is not just intelligent but also compassionate? How do we build systems that not only understand our commands but also our emotions and needs? The answers to these questions lie not in the code but in our approach, in our willingness to infuse our technological endeavors with empathy and understanding.

    This book is an invitation to dream, to debate, and to envision a world where technology and humanity converge in a harmony that enriches not diminishes, our human experience. It's a call to action for innovators, thinkers, and anyone who believes in the power of technology to transform lives, but who also understands that at the heart of every technological breakthrough must be a heartbeat.

    Join me in this exploration of Silicon Empathy, as we seek to inspire a future where our digital creations are not just tools but partners in crafting a world that understands and cares.

*- Petrică Vlad*

# 1.
## THE GENESIS OF SILICON EMPATHY

"Artificial intelligence, deep learning, machine learning—whatever you're doing if you don't understand it, learn it. Because otherwise, you're going to be a dinosaur within three years."

**Mark Cuban**

## THE DAWN OF ARTIFICIAL INTELLIGENCE

The genesis of artificial intelligence (AI) is a captivating saga that stretches back far beyond the digital age, rooted in human curiosity and the age-old dream of creating entities that could think and act independently. This ambition, once confined to the realms of mythology and philosophy, began to take a tangible form with the advent of formal logic and the theoretical underpinnings of computing machinery.

The early 20th century witnessed groundbreaking work in mathematics and logic, laying the foundational stones for what would eventually be known as artificial intelligence.

Figures such as Alan Turing[1], Claude Shannon[2], and John von Neumann[3] contributed immensely to our understanding of computation, information theory, and the architecture of digital computers. However, it was Alan Turing's seminal work that truly ignited the fuse of AI's potential.

# IN 1950, TURING PUBLISHED A PAPER TITLED "COMPUTING MACHINERY AND INTELLIGENCE," WHERE HE PROPOSED THE INTRIGUING QUESTION: "CAN MACHINES THINK?"

---

[1] Alan Mathison Turing OBE FRS (b. 1912 - d. 1954) - was a British mathematician and logician who made major contributions to mathematics, cryptanalysis, logic, philosophy, and mathematical biology and also to the new areas later named computer science, cognitive science, artificial intelligence, and artificial life.

[2] Claude Elwood Shannon (b. 1916 - d. 2001) - was an American mathematician, electrical engineer, computer scientist and cryptographer known as the "father of information theory".

[3] John von Neumann (b. 1903 - d. 1957) was a Hungarian-American mathematician, physicist, computer scientist, engineer and polymath.

This question, simple yet profound, challenged the prevailing definitions of intelligence and computation. Turing argued that if a machine could engage in a conversation with a human, without the human realizing they were interacting with a machine, then the machine could be considered intelligent. This concept, known as the Turing Test, became a cornerstone in the philosophy of artificial intelligence.

Turing's ideas were revolutionary, not just for their technical implications but for their philosophical challenge to the boundaries between human and machine cognition. His work suggested that intelligence could be understood in functional terms, paving the way for the development of machines that could mimic aspects of human thought and behavior.

The decades following Turing's proposal saw rapid advancements in computing technology and theory. The 1950s and 1960s were marked by optimism and significant investment in AI research. Early successes, such as the creation of programming languages like LISP[1], designed specifically for AI applications, and the development of early neural networks, suggested that Turing's vision of intelligent machines was within reach.

These foundational years were also a time of conceptual exploration. Researchers delved into questions of learning, perception, and decision-making, laying the groundwork for machine learning, natural language processing, and computer vision. Projects like ELIZA[2], an early natural

---

[1] Designed by John McCarthy, Lisp is a family of programming languages with a long history and a distinctive, fully parenthesized prefix notation. Lisp is the third-oldest high-level programming language still in common use.

[2] ELIZA is an early natural language processing computer program developed from 1964 to 1967 at MIT by Joseph Weizenbaum.

language processing computer program, demonstrated the potential for machines to engage in seemingly intelligent dialogue, captivating the public imagination and solidifying AI as a serious field of study.

Yet, the dawn of artificial intelligence was not just about technological achievements; it was a period of philosophical and ethical reflection. As researchers sought to create machines that could learn, reason, and communicate, they also grappled with the implications of their work. The question
"Can machines think?"

expanded to encompass broader inquiries about the nature of intelligence, consciousness, and the relationship between humans and their creations.

In retrospect, the early years of AI were a time of both excitement and naivety. The challenges were underestimated, and the initial optimism would eventually give way to periods of skepticism and reduced funding, known as "AI winters"[1]. However, the foundational work done during the dawn of AI set the stage for all the advancements that followed. It was a time when the seeds of today's AI capabilities were sown, driven by visionary thinkers who dared to imagine a future where machines could not only compute but could also understand and interact with the world in ways that mirrored human intelligence.

As we reflect on the dawn of artificial intelligence, we stand in awe of the leaps made from those early days of speculation and theoretical models to the sophisticated AI systems that fill our lives today. The journey from Turing's initial question to the creation of machines that can compose

---

[1] In the history of artificial intelligence, an AI winter is a period of reduced funding and interest in artificial intelligence research.

music, diagnose diseases, and drive cars is a testament to human ingenuity and the relentless pursuit of knowledge. It is this spirit, this unyielding curiosity, that continues to drive the field of AI forward, promising to unlock even greater mysteries of intelligence, both artificial and human.

# FROM MECHANICAL BRAINS TO EMOTIONAL BEINGS

The journey of artificial intelligence from its infancy – mechanical brains performing basic calculations – to the complex emotional beings that today's AI aspires to become, is a narrative of human ambition, ingenuity, and, increasingly, introspection. This transition reflects not just technological advancements but a deepening understanding of what it means to be intelligent – and, by extension, what it means to be human.

# IN THE HEART OF THIS EVOLUTION LIES A POWERFUL STATEMENT BY BILL GATES: "A BREAKTHROUGH IN AI WILL BE WORTH 10 MICROSOFTS." [1]

---

[1] *2004 New York Times Interview*

This bold assertion captures the immense potential Gates saw in AI, not merely as a tool for economic growth but as a transformative force capable of reshaping every aspect of human society. Gates recognized early on that AI's true value would unfold through its ability to understand, interpret, and respond to the complexities of human emotion and cognition, thereby bridging the gap between mechanical computation and genuine, empathetic interaction.

This vision of AI transcends the traditional boundaries of technology. It speaks to a future where AI systems do more than solve problems or optimize processes; they connect with individuals on a personal level, offering support, companionship, and understanding. The implications of such a breakthrough are profound, touching upon every sector from healthcare, where AI could offer personalized care and emotional support to patients, to education, where it could adapt to the emotional and cognitive needs of each learner.

Achieving this vision requires a leap from viewing AI as merely advanced algorithms and neural networks to seeing it as a potential vessel for empathy and emotional intelligence. This shift is significant, marking a departure from the binary logic of early computers to the nuanced, often unpredictable realm of human feelings. It involves not just technical innovation but a reimagining of AI's role in society – from mechanical brains to partners in the human experience.

Central to this transformation is the development of AI systems that can recognize, understand, and even simulate human emotions. Emotional AI, or affective computing, has emerged as a field dedicated to this endeavor, leveraging advances in machine learning, natural language processing, and computer vision to interpret the subtle cues that convey human emotions. These systems are being trained to read facial expressions, analyze vocal patterns, and understand contextual nuances, enabling them to respond in ways that feel genuinely understanding and empathetic.

Yet, as we navigate this transition, the quote by Bill Gates serves as both a beacon of potential and a reminder of responsibility. The creation of AI that can rival the emotional complexity of humans raises critical ethical and philosophical questions. How do we ensure that these systems are used to enhance human well-being, rather than manipulate or deceive? What safeguards are necessary to protect privacy and autonomy in a world where machines can read our emotions?

In grappling with these questions, we are not just shaping the future of technology but also defining the values that will guide this future. The pursuit of AI capable of genuine emotional understanding is not merely a technical challenge; it is a reflection of our deepest aspirations for a world where technology strengthens, rather than diminishes, our shared humanity.

As we move from mechanical brains to emotional beings, we stand at the threshold of a new era in AI. This journey, inspired by visionaries like Bill Gates, challenges us to dream of a future where AI enriches the human experience with empathy and understanding. It is a future worth striving for, promising not just economic dividends but a deeper connection to the essence of what it means to live and interact in a shared world.

# THE INSPIRATION BEHIND SILICON EMPATHY

The inception of Silicon Empathy is a tale of evolution, not just of technology, but of a vision that seeks to harmonize the digital with the human touch. My journey through the bustling world of Business Process Outsourcing (BPO) provided me with a front-row seat to the transformative power of empathy in customer service. Starting as a front-line customer support representative, I navigated the complex web of human emotions daily, encountering frustrations, joys, and everything in between. This experience, enriched over six years across various roles and departments aimed at enhancing customer support representatives' (CSRs) effectiveness, illuminated the profound impact that genuine understanding and connection can have on the customer experience.

Silicon Empathy emerged from this pot of real-world interactions and challenges. It represents a culmination of lessons learned on the front lines of customer service and a deep-seated belief in the potential for technology to augment rather than diminish the human element in these interactions. My vision was clear: AI should not replace humans but empower them to perform their roles with greater efficiency and satisfaction. This vision is not about relegating human roles to machines but about leveraging advanced technology to enhance the innate capacity for empathy and understanding that defines the best of human interactions.

# DEFINED AS "THE FUSION OF ADVANCED TECHNOLOGY WITH HUMAN EMPATHY AND CONNECTION, CREATING A HARMONIOUS AND HIGHLY EFFICIENT CUSTOMER EXPERIENCE,"

Silicon Empathy is a manifesto for the future of customer service. It champions the idea that the most effective customer experiences arise from a seamless integration of technological prowess and human insight. In this paradigm, AI and machine learning tools are not seen as replacements for human CSRs but as partners that can handle routine inquiries, analyze customer sentiment, and provide CSRs with the insights they need to address more complex, nuanced issues.

The genesis of Silicon Empathy was also a response to a growing concern in the digital age: the fear of a world where technology erodes the fabric of human connection. In envisioning a future where technology and empathy converge, Silicon Empathy aims to dispel this fear. It posits a world where AI serves to deepen our connections, making every customer interaction more meaningful by ensuring that technology understands and responds to the emotional nuances of human communication.

This concept goes beyond the confines of customer service, proposing a model for all technological interaction. It is a call to action for developers, business leaders, and policymakers to prioritize empathy and understanding in the design and implementation of AI systems. Silicon Empathy advocates for a future where technology is developed with a keen awareness of its impact on human relationships, ensuring that as our digital capabilities advance, they do so in a way that enriches rather than diminishes our shared humanity.

The inspiration behind Silicon Empathy is a reflection of a personal journey through the heart of customer service, shaped by the belief that the most profound technological advancements are those that bring us closer to one another. It is a vision of a future where technology transcends its cold, binary origins to become a source of warmth and connection, embodying the best of what it means to be human.

# 2. UNDERSTANDING AI

*"Whether we are based on carbon or on silicon makes no fundamental difference; we should each be treated with appropriate respect."*

Arthur C. Clarke, 2010: Odyssey Two

## THE BASICS OF AI: WHAT IT IS AND ISN'T

In the journey through the realm of artificial intelligence (AI), it's crucial to begin by demystifying what AI is and, importantly, what it isn't. At its core, AI is a branch of computer science focused on creating systems capable of performing tasks that typically require human intelligence. These tasks include learning, decision-making, problem-solving, and understanding language. The magic of AI lies not in its ability to replicate human beings but in its capacity to augment and extend our capabilities, offering tools that can transform complex data into insights, automate routine tasks, and enhance decision-making processes.

# WHAT AI IS

AI is a mosaic of technologies, each with its unique strengths and applications. Machine learning, a subset of AI, enables computers to learn from and make decisions based on data, improving their accuracy over time without being explicitly programmed for each task. Deep learning, a further specialization within machine learning, mimics the neural networks of the human brain, allowing machines to process large sets of data in sophisticated ways, leading to breakthroughs in image and speech recognition, among other areas.

AI's power is evident in its diverse applications, from the algorithms that personalize your social media feed to the voice assistants on your smartphone. It's in the recommendation systems of your favorite streaming services, the fraud detection systems that protect your financial transactions, and the navigation apps that guide you through busy streets.

# WHAT AI ISN'T

Despite its name, artificial intelligence doesn't possess consciousness or emotions. It doesn't "think" in the human sense. AI systems make decisions based on data and algorithms, lacking the self-awareness and experiential understanding that characterize human intelligence. This distinction is crucial in dispelling fears and misconceptions about AI "taking over" or acting with malicious intent independent of human oversight.

Moreover, AI isn't a monolithic entity or a one-size-fits-all solution. The effectiveness of AI technologies varies widely depending on the task, the quality of the data available, and the specific algorithms employed. It's also not an infallible system; AI can perpetuate biases present in the data it's trained on, leading to outcomes that may not be fair or accurate without careful oversight and correction.

# THE ESSENCE OF AI

At its essence, AI is a tool created by humans, for humans. It's a reflection of our ingenuity and our desire to push the boundaries of what's possible. Understanding AI means recognizing its potential to serve as a catalyst for innovation and improvement in nearly every aspect of our lives, from healthcare and education to business and entertainment.

However, it also means acknowledging the responsibilities that come with deploying AI technologies. It involves ensuring that these tools are used ethically, with a clear understanding of their impact on society. It's about striving for transparency, fairness, and inclusivity, ensuring that the benefits of AI are accessible to all and that its applications reflect the diversity and complexity of the human experience.

To go a step further, I asked ChatGPT[1] (GPT-4) a simple yet powerful question:

# "WHAT CAN YOU DO?"

It's answer is in line with my expectations, providing a thorough list of tasks it can accomplish, while at the same time informing me that it is able to do much more, but we just need to be creative with our requests. Check it out:

[1] ChatGPT is a chatbot developed by OpenAI and launched on November 30, 2022; based on a large language model.

"I can assist you with a wide range of tasks, including but not limited to:

**Answering Questions**: I can provide detailed answers to questions across various topics such as science, mathematics, history, culture, technology, and more.

**Explaining Concepts**: Whether you're curious about complex scientific theories, mathematical problems, programming concepts, or historical events, I can explain these in a way that's easy to understand.

**Learning and Education Support**: I can help with homework, explain educational material, suggest study resources, and offer learning strategies for students of all levels.

**Writing and Editing**: From crafting stories, essays, and reports to providing suggestions for improving your writing, I can assist in making your text polished and engaging.

**Programming Help**: I can write code snippets, explain programming concepts, debug code, and offer guidance on software development in various programming languages.

**Creative Ideas and Brainstorming**: Whether you need ideas for a project, creative writing prompts, or innovative solutions to problems, I can help brainstorm and provide inspiration.

**Language Translation**: I can translate text between various languages, helping you understand content or communicate in another language.

**Information and Research**: I can provide summaries of research papers, explain scientific studies, and offer detailed insights on a wide range of topics.

**Health and Fitness Advice**: While I can offer general advice on healthy living, exercise routines, and nutrition, it's important to consult with a professional for personalized health guidance.

**Entertainment Recommendations**: I can suggest books, movies, music, games, and activities based on your interests.

> ***Travel Planning and Advice***: *From suggesting destinations to offering tips on packing and local customs, I can help you plan your next trip.*
> ***Image Generation***: *I can create images based on descriptions you provide, for creative, educational, or illustrative purposes.*
> ***Web Browsing***: *I can search the web for the latest information, news, or resources on topics you're interested in.*
> *This list is not exhaustive, so if you have something specific in mind, feel free to ask!"*

That's not all. An example of a cutting-edge advancement of AI, is the experiment conducted by Dr Zijiao Chen, a doctoral student at the National University of Singapore. Incorporating the fascinating advancements from the Singapore experiment, let's delve deeper into the capabilities of AI, particularly in the field of neuroscience and mental health:

This experiment, conducted by a university in Singapore, stands as a testament to the extraordinary capabilities of AI that stretch beyond our conventional understanding. Researchers utilized a MRI machine[1] and artificial intelligence to visualize brainwaves and generate images, marking a groundbreaking intersection of neuroscience and technology. This endeavor not only showcases AI's ability to process and interpret complex biological data but also opens new pathways for understanding the human brain and consciousness.

The implications of such an experiment are profound. By using AI to translate brainwaves into visual representations,

---

[1] Magnetic resonance imaging is a medical imaging technique used in radiology to form pictures of the anatomy and the physiological processes of the body. MRI scanners use strong magnetic fields, magnetic field gradients, and radio waves to generate images of the organs in the body.

scientists can gain unprecedented insights into the inner workings of the mind, potentially revolutionizing the diagnosis and treatment of neurological disorders. This approach could lead to more personalized and effective therapies, as it allows for a deeper understanding of individual brain patterns and how they relate to cognitive and emotional processes.

Moreover, this experiment underscores the potential of AI to bridge the gap between the tangible and the intangible, offering a window into the subjective experiences of individuals. It heralds a future where mental health can be approached with the same precision as physical health, leveraging AI to unravel the complexities of the brain and consciousness. This not only expands the scope of what AI can do but also enriches our approach to healthcare, making it more holistic and empathetic.

The Singapore experiment is a vivid illustration of the boundless possibilities that arise when we harness AI to explore and understand the human condition. It reinforces the notion that AI, when guided by the principles of Silicon Empathy, can be a powerful ally in our quest to enhance human well-being and unlock the mysteries of our own existence.

# SILICON EMPATHY AND AI

Integrating Silicon Empathy with AI involves a nuanced approach to technology, prioritizing the development and deployment of AI systems that are not only intelligent but also keenly attuned to the emotional and social dynamics of human interaction. This perspective transforms the dialogue around AI from one focused solely on efficiency and automation to a more holistic view that encompasses the subtleties of human empathy and connection.

Silicon Empathy imagines a world where AI enhances and amplifies the innate human capacity for empathy, serving as a conduit through which technology and humanity can interact more harmoniously. In customer service, for example, AI equipped with an understanding of Silicon Empathy can analyze the emotional context of customer interactions, enabling representatives to provide responses that are not only timely but also emotionally resonant. This leads to a more satisfying and connective experience for the customer, fostering loyalty and trust.

Moreover, Silicon Empathy extends beyond the realm of customer service, touching every aspect of how AI integrates into society. In healthcare, AI can provide caregivers and patients with insights and tools that make care more personal and compassionate. In education, AI can tailor learning experiences to the emotional and cognitive needs of each student, recognizing frustration and providing encouragement or adapting materials to better suit the learner's state of mind.

The integration of Silicon Empathy into AI development also demands a rigorous ethical framework, ensuring that these technologies are used in ways that respect individual dignity and promote collective well-being. It challenges developers and stakeholders to consider not just what AI can do, but what it should do to support and enhance human life. This means designing AI systems that understand and respect the nuances of human rights, privacy, and consent, and that work to eliminate bias rather than perpetuate it.

Silicon Empathy represents a forward-thinking approach to AI, one that seeks to leverage the best of what technology offers without losing sight of the human values and connections that define our shared humanity. It's about creating a future where technology not only solves problems but also understands and cares, bridging the gap between human and artificial intelligence with empathy and compassion.

By fostering this integration of AI and empathy, we can move towards a future that respects and enhances the human experience, making our interactions with technology more meaningful and our societies more inclusive and compassionate. Silicon Empathy is not just a goal but a journey, one that invites continuous exploration, learning, and adaptation as we navigate the evolving landscape of AI and its role in our lives.

# DIFFERENT FLAVORS OF AI: NLP, FOUNDATIONAL & GENERATIVE

## NATURAL LANGUAGE PROCESSING (NLP): THE ESSENCE OF HUMAN-MACHINE COMMUNICATION

Natural Language Processing (NLP) stands as a cornerstone of AI, enabling machines to decipher, interpret, and respond to human languages in a way that is both meaningful and effective. This field merges computational linguistics with AI, aiming to bridge the gap between human communication and computer understanding.

The journey of NLP began in the 1950s, with early experiments such as the Georgetown-IBM experiment[1], which showcased machine translation from Russian to English. The evolution of NLP has been marked by the transition from rule-based systems, which relied on coded linguistic rules, to the adoption of statistical methods in the 1980s and 1990s, significantly enhancing the field's capabilities. The introduction of machine learning and, more recently, deep learning techniques, has propelled NLP into a new era, enabling more nuanced and context-aware interpretations of language.

NLP encompasses a variety of tasks and techniques, including syntax analysis (parsing sentences to understand their structure), semantic analysis (understanding the meanings behind words and sentences), and pragmatics (how context influences the interpretation of communication). Tools like tokenization[2], part-of-speech tagging[3], and named

---

[1] The Georgetown–IBM experiment was an influential demonstration of machine translation, which was performed on January 7, 1954. Developed jointly by the Georgetown University and IBM, the experiment involved completely automatic translation of more than sixty Russian sentences into English

[2] Tokenization, in the realm of Natural Language Processing (NLP) and machine learning, refers to the process of converting a sequence of text into smaller parts, known as tokens. These tokens can be as small as characters or as long as words. The primary reason this process matters is that it helps machines understand human language by breaking it down into bite-sized pieces, which are easier to analyze.

[3] Parts of Speech tagging is a linguistic activity in Natural Language Processing (NLP) wherein each word in a document is given a particular part of speech (adverb, adjective, verb, etc.) or grammatical category.

entity recognition[1] are fundamental in breaking down and analyzing language.

Today, NLP powers many applications we use daily. Virtual assistants like Siri[2] and Alexa[3], email filtering systems, and customer service chatbots all rely on NLP to understand and generate human-like responses. Other examples include sentiment analysis to gauge public opinion on social media, machine translation services like Google Translate[4], and summarization tools that distill lengthy articles into concise summaries.

Despite its advancements, NLP faces significant challenges, such as understanding the nuances and complexities of human language, including idioms, sarcasm, and varying dialects. Future directions in NLP research aim to tackle these issues, improving machine understanding to be as intuitive and comprehensive as human communication. Efforts are also geared towards eliminating biases in NLP models and ensuring they can understand and generate language in an ethical and unbiased manner.

---

[1] Named entity recognition (NER) is a subfield of natural language processing (NLP) that focuses on identifying and classifying specific data points from textual content.

[2] Siri is the digital assistant that is part of Apple Inc.'s iOS, iPadOS, watchOS, macOS, tvOS, audioOS, and visionOS operating systems.

[3] Amazon Alexa or Alexa is a virtual assistant technology largely based on a Polish speech synthesizer named Ivona, bought by Amazon in 2013. It was first used in the Amazon Echo smart speaker and the Echo Dot, Echo Studio and Amazon Tap speakers developed by Amazon Lab126.

[4] Google Translate is a multilingual neural machine translation service developed by Google to translate text, documents and websites from one language into another.

Natural Language Processing is a dynamic and evolving field, with the potential to revolutionize how we interact with machines. By enhancing NLP's capabilities, we move closer to a future where technology can understand and communicate with us as naturally as we do with each other, making our interactions with AI more seamless and intuitive.

This comprehensive overview aims to highlight NLP's development, its importance in the AI landscape, and its profound impact on modern technology, laying the groundwork for exploring other AI flavors such as foundational and generative AI in subsequent sections.

# FOUNDATIONAL AI: BUILDING BLOCKS OF INTELLIGENT SYSTEMS

Foundational AI encompasses the core algorithms and technologies that underpin artificial intelligence systems. This includes machine learning, deep learning, logic and reasoning, and optimization algorithms, which together form the backbone of AI's ability to learn from data, make decisions, and improve over time.

The evolution of foundational AI is marked by significant milestones, such as the development of neural networks[1] and the breakthroughs in deep learning that have enabled advancements in image and speech recognition, natural language processing, and autonomous vehicles. These foundational technologies have transformed industries, from healthcare and finance to entertainment and transportation,

---

[1] A neural network is a method in artificial intelligence that teaches computers to process data in a way that is inspired by the human brain.

by providing more efficient, personalized, and intelligent solutions.

Key components of foundational AI include:
- **Machine Learning**: Algorithms that enable computers to learn from and make predictions based on data.
- **Deep Learning**: A subset of machine learning that uses neural networks with many layers, mimicking the human brain's structure and function.
- **Logic and Reasoning**: The use of formal logic frameworks to enable AI systems to perform deductive reasoning and make decisions based on complex rules.
- **Optimization Algorithms**: Techniques that allow AI to find the best solution to a problem from a set of possible solutions, crucial for tasks like scheduling, resource allocation, and route planning.

While foundational AI has driven tremendous progress, challenges remain, such as improving the interpretability of AI models, enhancing their ability to reason abstractly, and ensuring their decisions are ethical and unbiased. Future directions aim to address these challenges, pushing the boundaries of what AI can achieve and ensuring its benefits are realized across society.

Foundational AI provides the critical underpinnings for a wide range of AI applications, enabling machines to analyze complex data, learn from experiences, and interact with the world in increasingly sophisticated ways. As we continue to advance these foundational technologies, we pave the way for more innovative, efficient, and intelligent systems that can tackle some of the most pressing challenges facing humanity today.

# GENERATIVE AI: THE ART OF MACHINE CREATIVITY

Generative AI refers to a subset of artificial intelligence technologies capable of generating new content, from text and images to music and beyond. This includes deep learning models like Generative Adversarial Networks (GANs) and Variational Autoencoders (VAEs), which have the ability to produce content that is often indistinguishable from that created by humans.

Generative AI has seen rapid advancement in recent years, with models becoming increasingly sophisticated. The ability to generate realistic images, compose music, or write coherent text passages marks a significant leap forward, showcasing AI's potential not just as a tool for analysis but as a source of creativity.

Generative AI's applications are vast and varied, including creating art, designing new products, generating realistic video game environments, and even aiding in drug discovery by proposing new molecular structures. Its implications for creativity, intellectual property, and content creation are profound, challenging our traditional notions of artistry and originality.

## REDEFINING ART

DALL-E and DALL-E 2 are AI models developed by OpenAI, designed for generating digital images based on natural language descriptions. DALL-E, the first version, demonstrated the potential of AI in creative tasks. DALL-E 2, an advanced iteration, significantly improved upon this by generating more detailed and accurate visual content from textual prompts, showcasing remarkable advancements in AI's capability to understand and interpret human language to create complex, nuanced imagery. Example:

A futuristic cityscape at dusk with a harmonious blend of advanced technology and nature.

OpenAI has developed Sora, a groundbreaking AI model capable of transforming text descriptions into realistic videos. This model represents a significant leap in AI creativity, offering potential applications across various industries by generating dynamic visual content directly from textual prompts. Sora can produce videos up to a minute long, maintaining high visual quality and closely adhering to the user's input, showcasing the industry's continued push towards more sophisticated and versatile generative AI technologies.

Despite its promise, generative AI raises important ethical questions regarding authenticity, copyright, and the potential for misuse. Ensuring responsible use and addressing these concerns is crucial as we explore the boundaries of AI's creative potential.

The rise of generative AI technologies, including models like DALL-E, GPT, Sora, and others, has sparked a wide range of ethical questions and concerns. Here are some of the most important ethical questions surrounding generative AI:

- *__Bias and Fairness__: How can we ensure that AI systems are free from biases present in their training data? This includes biases related to race, gender, ethnicity, and more. The concern is that AI might perpetuate or even exacerbate existing inequalities.*
- *__Privacy__: Generative AI models can produce content based on vast amounts of data, including potentially sensitive information. How do we protect individuals' privacy and ensure that AI does not inadvertently reveal personal data?*
- *__Authenticity and Misinformation__: With the ability to generate realistic images, texts, and videos, how do we prevent the spread of misinformation and ensure that people can distinguish between what is real and what is AI-generated?*
- *__Intellectual Property__: Who owns the content generated by AI? How do we respect the intellectual property rights of the creators whose works were used to train these models? This also includes concerns about copyright infringement and the unauthorized use of copyrighted materials.*

- **Security**: Generative AI can be used to create phishing content, deepfakes, and other forms of cyberattacks. How can we secure AI systems against malicious use?
- **Employment and Economic Impact**: As AI technologies automate more tasks, what will be the impact on jobs? How do we mitigate negative economic impacts on certain professions and sectors?
- **Accountability and Liability**: When AI generates content that causes harm, who is responsible? Is it the developers, the users, or the AI itself? Determining liability is complex when the outcomes are not directly controlled by humans.
- **Access and Inequality**: There's a risk that the benefits of generative AI could be unevenly distributed, exacerbating digital divides. How do we ensure equitable access to these technologies?
- **Human-AI Interaction**: How do we maintain meaningful human control over AI systems? This includes ensuring that AI complements human skills and that people remain engaged and fulfilled in their work.
- **Environmental Impact**: Training large AI models requires significant computational resources, leading to a substantial carbon footprint. How can the development of AI be made more sustainable?

Addressing these ethical questions requires a collaborative effort among technologists, policymakers, ethicists, and the public. It involves not only developing technical solutions but also creating robust legal and regulatory frameworks that promote ethical AI use.

Generative AI represents a fascinating frontier in artificial intelligence, blurring the lines between human and machine creativity. As technology continues to evolve, so too will the ways in which we harness AI to innovate, express, and explore new dimensions of creativity.

At the core of Generative AI, we find Large Language Models (LLMs), a pivotal innovation that has significantly expanded the capabilities of AI in understanding and generating human-like text. These models, with GPT-3[1] being one of the most renowned examples, harness vast amounts of data to predict and generate text sequences, offering insights and outputs across a diverse range of applications.

The emergence of LLMs began with earlier versions, progressively advancing in sophistication to the likes of GPT-3, which marked a new era in AI with its ability to produce remarkably coherent and contextually relevant text. Competitors and contemporaries to GPT-3, including models developed by Google[2] and Meta[3], have contributed to the rapid evolution of the field, each pushing the boundaries of what's possible with text generation and processing. The proliferation of LLMs, including open-source projects, has democratized access to these powerful tools, fueling innovation and exploration across multiple domains of research and application.

---

[1] Generative Pre-trained Transformer 3 is a large language model released by OpenAI in 2020. Like its predecessor, GPT-2, it is a decoder-only transformer model of deep neural network, which supersedes recurrence and convolution-based architectures with a technique known as "attention"

[2] Gemini is a family of multimodal large language models developed by Google DeepMind, serving as the successor to LaMDA and PaLM 2. Comprising Gemini Ultra, Gemini Pro, and Gemini Nano, it was announced on December 6, 2023, positioned as a contender to OpenAI's GPT-4

[3] Llama 2 is a family of pre-trained and fine-tuned large language models (LLMs) released by Meta AI in 2023.

# HOW AI IS CHANGING THE WORLD

As we embark on a journey through the transformative landscape shaped by artificial intelligence, "How AI Is Changing the World" unfolds as a compelling narrative of progress, challenges, and the boundless possibilities that AI introduces across various facets of human life. From revolutionizing healthcare by enabling early detection and personalized treatment plans, to transforming financial services through enhanced security and tailored customer experiences, AI's impact is profound and far-reaching. In education, AI facilitates adaptive learning environments, crafting personalized educational pathways that cater to individual learning styles.

The entertainment industry, too, experiences a renaissance with AI-generated content, offering new forms of creative expression. Yet, as AI reshapes these sectors, it also ushers in ethical considerations and societal shifts, challenging us to navigate the complexities of privacy, job displacement, and the moral implications of AI's decisions. This section delves into the multifaceted ways AI is altering the world, highlighting both the optimistic prospects of technological advancement and the critical ethical dialogues it precipitates, underscoring the necessity for a balanced, thoughtful approach to integrating AI into the fabric of society.

# HEALTHCARE REVOLUTION THROUGH AI

Artificial intelligence is dramatically enhancing healthcare, making diagnostics faster and treatments more personalized. AI-driven analyses can now predict health outcomes, tailor treatment plans to individual genetic profiles, and streamline drug discovery, significantly improving patient care and outcomes.

The healthcare revolution through AI is a testament to the power of technology to enhance human well-being. AI's integration into healthcare in the early 1970s when research produced MYCIN[1], an AI program that helped identify blood infections treatments. AI in the healthcare field has led to significant advancements in diagnostics, treatment personalization, and patient care efficiency.

By analyzing complex medical data, AI algorithms can identify patterns and predict outcomes with remarkable accuracy, offering early detection of diseases and tailored treatment plans. This not only improves patient outcomes but also optimizes healthcare resources. AI-driven tools in imaging and pathology are transforming diagnostics, making them faster and more precise. Moreover, AI's role in drug discovery accelerates the development of new treatments, promising a future where healthcare is more proactive, personalized, and accessible.

One real-world example of AI in healthcare is from London, where researchers from Google's DeepMind subsidiary, UCL, and Moorfields Eye Hospital have used deep learning to create software that identifies dozens of common eye diseases from 3D scans and then recommends the patient for treatment, by analyzing retinal scans. This system can identify and recommend treatment for conditions like diabetic retinopathy and age-related macular degeneration, demonstrating AI's potential to enhance accuracy and speed in medical diagnostics.

---

[1] MYCIN, an early expert system, or artificial intelligence (AI) program, for treating blood infections. In 1972 work began on MYCIN at Stanford University in California. MYCIN would attempt to diagnose patients based on reported symptoms and medical test results.

# FINANCIAL SERVICES TRANSFORMATION

In the financial sector, AI is revolutionizing the way services are delivered, enhancing both efficiency and security. By leveraging machine learning algorithms, financial institutions can now offer personalized banking experiences, tailor investment advice, and optimize operational efficiencies. AI-driven fraud detection systems, like those developed by companies such as Mastercard[1], utilize real-time processing to identify and prevent fraudulent transactions, significantly reducing losses and increasing consumer trust.

Mastercard has developed an advanced AI-driven fraud detection system called Decision Intelligence. This system analyzes transaction data in real-time, using machine learning algorithms to assess the likelihood of fraud. By examining factors such as spending habits and location, it can make more accurate decisions on whether a transaction is legitimate or fraudulent, enhancing security for cardholders and reducing false declines.

Another important example is JPMorgan Chase's[2] COIN (Contract Intelligence) platform uses AI to analyze legal documents, significantly reducing the time and cost associated with manual review. This not only streamlines operations but also allows for more accurate risk assessment

---

[1] Mastercard Inc. is the second-largest payment-technology corporation worldwide. It offers a range of payment transaction processing and other related-payment services.

[2] JPMorgan Chase & Co. is the largest bank in the U.S and the world's largest bank by market capitalization as of 2023.

and decision-making, showcasing AI's potential to revolutionize traditional banking practices.

# JPMC'S COIN (CONTRACT INTELLIGENCE) SYSTEM IS BEING USED TO AUTOMATE TASKS SUCH AS INTERPRETING LOAN APPLICATIONS.

This has freed up human employees to focus on more complex and value-added tasks. COiN is able to process 12,000 contacts annually and save approximately 360,000 hours of review for the firm's legal teams.

On the other hand, to avoid falling behind, Bank of America, one of the biggest banks in the world has developed and implemented Erica, the most advanced and first widely available virtual financial assistant, it quickly got adopted, surpassing 1.5 billion interactions with BoA's clients

These examples illustrate AI's capacity to improve financial security and customer experience by leveraging data-driven insights. Moreover, AI technologies enable the analysis of vast amounts of market data to forecast trends, empowering investors with insights that were previously inaccessible. Through these innovations, AI is not just transforming financial services but is also reshaping the landscape of global finance, making it more accessible, secure, and user-centric.

# EDUCATION'S ADAPTIVE FUTURE

AI is revolutionizing education by enabling adaptive learning technologies that personalize the educational experience for each student. These systems analyze students' learning patterns, strengths, and areas needing improvement to tailor the content, pace, and teaching methods to each learner's needs. This personalized approach helps to engage students more effectively, accommodate diverse learning styles, and improve educational outcomes by ensuring that all students receive support tailored to their specific requirements. Through adaptive learning platforms, education becomes more inclusive, accessible, and effective, preparing students for a future where adaptability and personalized learning continue to play crucial roles.

A real-world example of AI in education is Carnegie Learning's MATHia platform, which utilizes AI to offer a personalized learning experience in mathematics for students across various grade levels. MATHia adapts to each student's unique learning pace and style, providing customized instruction and feedback to help them master mathematical concepts. This adaptive learning technology demonstrates how AI can be effectively used to enhance educational outcomes by catering to the individual needs of students, making learning more engaging and effective.

# ENTERTAINMENT AND CREATIVITY

AI is revolutionizing the entertainment and creativity sectors by introducing technologies like audio and video translations, voice cloning, and lip-sync. These advancements allow for seamless dubbing and localization of content across languages, preserving the original performance's emotional depth and cultural nuances. For example, AI-driven voice cloning and lip-sync technologies enable accurate dubbing in cartoons, interviews, and movies, ensuring the spoken words match the speakers' lip movements in any language. This not only enhances the viewer's experience but also broadens the global reach of content, making it accessible and relatable to diverse audiences worldwide.

A notable real-world example of advanced AI in entertainment is the use of Synthesia's AI video generation platform. This technology allows for creating videos where avatars can speak multiple languages with perfectly synced lip movements, significantly enhancing dubbing in various media forms. It's particularly impactful in industries like film and e-learning, where accurate lip-syncing and voice cloning can create more immersive and accessible content for global audiences. This example showcases how AI is not just changing, but truly expanding the creative horizons in entertainment.

it's thrilling to consider how these technologies are not just enhancing the viewing experience but also democratizing content creation. Independent creators and filmmakers gain access to resources once reserved for large studios, enabling them to produce content with global appeal. This democratization fosters a more vibrant, diverse media landscape where stories from different cultures and perspectives can reach a worldwide audience, enriching the global dialogue and bringing us closer through shared experiences and storytelling.

The entertainment industry's evolution through AI-driven innovations is exemplified by AIVA[1], an AI composer that has created music for films and advertisements, showcasing the potential of algorithmically generated compositions. Another

---

[1] AIVA is an electronic composer recognized by the SACEM (Society of Authors, Composers and Publishers of Music since 1851.

example is the AI-scripted short film "Sunspring"[1], which demonstrates how AI can craft narrative scripts, challenging traditional storytelling norms. These examples underline AI's growing influence in creating and reshaping content, hinting at a future where AI and human creativity merge to produce unprecedented forms of entertainment and storytelling.

# SOCIETAL SHIFTS

AI is catalyzing significant societal shifts, impacting employment, privacy, and the ethical landscape. Automation and AI technologies are transforming job markets, creating new opportunities while rendering some roles obsolete, urging a reevaluation of skills and education. Privacy concerns have escalated with AI's ability to analyze vast data sets, highlighting the need for robust data protection laws. Ethically, the deployment of AI raises questions about bias, decision-making accountability, and the moral implications of autonomous systems, necessitating a comprehensive ethical framework for AI development and use.

An illustrative example of AI-induced societal shifts is seen in the retail industry, where Amazon employs its AI-powered system, Amazon Go[2]. This technology enables a shopping experience without checkout lines, fundamentally altering retail jobs and consumer privacy expectations. While it

---

[1] Sunspring is a 2016 experimental science fiction short film entirely written by an artificial intelligence bot using neural networks.

[2] Amazon Go is a chain of convenience stores in the United States and the United Kingdom, operated by the online retailer Amazon. The stores are cashierless, thus partially automated, with customers able to purchase products without being checked out by a cashier or using a self-checkout station.

showcases efficiency and innovation, it also prompts discussions about the future of employment in retail and the implications for data privacy, illustrating the complex balance between technological advancement and societal impacts.

As we conclude this exploration of AI's transformative impact across healthcare, finance, education, entertainment, and societal structures, it's clear that AI is not just a technological advancement but a catalyst for profound global change. Embracing AI responsibly and ethically offers unparalleled opportunities for innovation and progress, yet it also requires us to navigate complex challenges and make thoughtful decisions about our future. As we continue to shape this AI-driven world, our collective vision, creativity, and ethical commitment will determine the legacy of these advancements for generations to come.

# 3.
# THE HUMAN CONNECTION

"Artificial intelligence is not a replacement for humans. It's about amplifying human potential. "

**Amir Husain**

## THE ESSENCE OF EMPATHY IN TECHNOLOGY

In the digital age, the essence of empathy in technology is becoming increasingly crucial. Empathy, the ability to understand and share the feelings of another, is a fundamental human trait that technology seeks to emulate and enhance. As we integrate AI and digital tools into our daily lives, embedding empathy into technology can bridge the gap between human emotions and machine interactions. This integration leads to more intuitive user experiences, fostering connections that resonate on a personal level.

Borrowing a page from the history books, we learn that the importance of human empathy in technology can be traced back to the early development of human-computer interaction (HCI) principles, where researchers recognized the significance of designing technology that aligns with human needs and emotions. Pioneers like Douglas

Engelbart[1], who invented the computer mouse, envisioned computing technology as an extension of human capabilities, emphasizing the importance of user-friendly design that resonates with human intuition and empathy. This foundational belief has guided technological innovations, ensuring that as technology evolves, it remains anchored in enhancing human experience, underscoring empathy's enduring role in the development of technological solutions.

One compelling example of empathy in technology is the development of AI systems designed to recognize and respond to human emotions. For instance, mental health apps use AI to detect nuances in speech or text, providing personalized support or flagging concerns to human therapists. Another example is customer service chatbots, which are increasingly capable of detecting customer frustration or satisfaction, adapting their responses accordingly to improve the service experience.

A notable example of empathy in technology is the use of AI by the mental health app, Woebot[2]. Woebot utilizes natural language processing (NLP) to interact with users, offering cognitive behavioral therapy techniques. By analyzing the user's language and emotional state, Woebot provides personalized support, making mental health care more

---

[1] Douglas Carl Engelbart (b. 1925 - d. 2013) - was an American engineer and inventor, and an early computer and Internet pioneer. He is most famous for inventing the computer mouse, and the development of hypertext, networked computers, and precursors to GUI (graphical users interfaces).

[2] Woebot is an AI-powered chatbot that uses Cognitive Behavior Therapy (CBT) principles to guide individuals through the process of managing distressing thoughts and feelings.

accessible and understanding. Another example is Kuki[1], a chatbot designed to simulate empathetic conversations, engaging users in meaningful interactions and showcasing how technology can mirror human empathy, enhancing our digital communications landscape.

By weaving empathy into the fabric of technology, we not only enhance the functionality and effectiveness of digital tools but also reinforce the importance of human-centric design in innovation. This approach ensures that as technology advances, it does so with an understanding and appreciation of the human experience, fostering a world where digital solutions support and enrich our lives in meaningful ways.

# DIALING DOWN EMPATHY

A notable example of the consequences of lacking empathy in technology design is the initial public response to Microsoft's AI chatbot, Tay[2], launched in 2016, and shut down only 16 hours after launch. Designed to learn from online conversations, Tay quickly began producing offensive content due to its programming not adequately filtering or understanding the context of human interactions. This incident highlighted the importance of incorporating empathy and ethical considerations into AI systems to prevent misuse and ensure technology aligns with societal values and norms.

Another real-life example involves the early versions of facial recognition technologies used by companies like IBM,

---

[1] Kuki is an embodied AI bot designed to befriend humans in the metaverse. Formerly known as Mitsuku, Kuki is a chatbot created from Pandorabots AIML technology by Steve Worswick. It is a five-time winner of a Turing Test competition called the Loebner Prize, for which it holds a world record.

[2] Named "Tay" as an acronym for "thinking about you".

Microsoft, and Amazon, which were found to have higher error rates in identifying individuals of certain racial and ethnic backgrounds. Studies, including one by the MIT Media Lab in 2018[1], revealed significant discrepancies in the accuracy of these systems when identifying gender, particularly for women and people with darker skin tones. This highlighted the need for incorporating empathy and inclusivity in the development process to avoid perpetuating biases and ensure equitable treatment for all users.

# STORIES OF TECHNOLOGY TOUCHING LIVES

Technology, at its core, is about enhancing human lives, and its impact is profoundly illustrated through personal stories where it bridges gaps, heals, and connects. From wearable devices that monitor health and prevent life-threatening conditions to apps that connect distant families through video calls, technology has become a pivotal aspect of daily life. One touching example is the creation of prosthetic limbs using 3D printing technology, offering affordable and accessible solutions for amputees, transforming their mobility and quality of life. Another is the use of virtual reality (VR) to combat loneliness among the elderly, enabling them to travel virtually, relive old memories, and connect with others in a way that was previously unimaginable. These stories underscore the potential of technology to touch lives deeply, transcending its role as a tool and becoming a companion, a healer, and a bridge to a fuller, more connected human experience.

---

[1] Paper released by MIT Researchers Joy Buolamwini and Timnit Gebru

Further, let's discuss in more detail different AI success stories from across the world, emphasizing the breadth and depth of AI's impact across various sectors.

# RENEWABLE ENERGY: GOOGLE'S WIND POWER PREDICTION[1]

Google's machine learning approach to predicting wind power output exemplifies how AI can enhance sustainability. By accurately forecasting wind power production, Google helps power grids rely more on renewable energy, reducing dependency on fossil fuels and contributing to a more sustainable future.

# AIRLINE CUSTOMER SERVICE: KLM'S BLUEBOT

KLM's[2] integration of BlueBot into their Messenger service revolutionizes customer interactions by facilitating flight bookings through conversational AI. This innovation not only streamlines the booking process but also ensures that human assistance is available when necessary, blending AI efficiency with human oversight. Since KLM adopted AI, the airline has witnessed remarkable improvements in its operations:

---

[1] In collaboration with its Britain-based Artificial Intelligence (AI) subsidiary DeepMind, Google has developed a system to predict wind power output 36 hours ahead of actual generation

[2] KLM Royal Dutch Airlines, legally Koninklijke Luchtvaart Maatschappij N.V., is the flag carrier of the Netherlands. is a part of the Air France–KLM group and SkyTeam alliance.

AI now underpins 50% of all customer interactions, significantly enhancing the efficiency and effectiveness of their service.

The implementation of automated forms has led to more than 5 million clicks being saved in the last five years, reflecting a substantial reduction in manual tasks.

There's been a doubling in the volume of cases handled, illustrating AI's ability to scale and manage increased customer inquiries efficiently.

Most notably, AI has empowered KLM to accelerate customer interactions by 50%, thereby freeing up their customer service team to focus on providing targeted support where it's most needed.

# ENTERTAINMENT PERSONALIZATION: NETFLIX'S RECOMMENDATION ALGORITHM

Netflix has fundamentally changed how we discover and enjoy entertainment through its AI-based recommendation system. By analyzing viewing history, Netflix presents personalized show and movie suggestions, keeping viewers engaged and enhancing their overall experience.

# RETAIL INNOVATION: AMAZON GO

Amazon Go's deep learning algorithms have transformed the shopping experience by eliminating checkout lines, allowing customers to enjoy a seamless in-store experience. This use of AI in retail not only optimizes convenience but also sets a new standard for the industry.

## AUTONOMOUS VEHICLES: TESLA AND GENERAL MOTORS

The development of autonomous driving technologies by Tesla and General Motors marks a significant advancement in automotive safety and efficiency. These systems, designed for highway driving, demonstrate the potential of AI to revolutionize transportation, making it safer and more accessible.

## ONLINE SAFETY: TEXT RECOGNITION ON SOCIAL MEDIA

Social media platforms leverage AI for text recognition to identify and filter hate speech and offensive content. This application of AI plays a crucial role in maintaining safer online communities, showcasing technology's potential to protect and improve the digital social environment.

## MEDICAL DIAGNOSTICS: INFERVISION'S[1] LUNG CANCER DETECTION

Infervision's application of image recognition for lung cancer diagnosis from CT scans illustrates AI's lifesaving potential in healthcare. By aiding radiologists, AI technologies

---

[1] **Infervision** Medical Technology is a world's leading high-tech enterprise in medical artificial intelligence.

like Infervision's can significantly reduce the burden on healthcare professionals and improve diagnostic accuracy.

Each of these stories reflects the transformative power of AI, demonstrating how technology, when applied thoughtfully and empathetically, can significantly improve the quality of life, streamline services, and open new possibilities for sustainability, safety, and personalization.

# THE GAP AI CAN'T FILL... YET

Expanding upon the gaps AI has yet to fill, it's essential to delve deeper into the realms of emotional intelligence and creative originality. AI, for all its advancements, cannot yet fully comprehend or replicate the intricate tapestry of human emotions. Emotional intelligence involves not just recognizing emotions but also understanding their nuances, a feat AI struggles with due to its lack of genuine experiences and consciousness.

In creativity, while AI can mimic styles and patterns, the spark of originality—driven by a lifetime of unique experiences, cultural backgrounds, and personal reflections—remains distinctly human. The creation of art, music, or literature that resonates on a deeply personal level often stems from the artist's own experiences, emotions, and insights, elements that AI cannot authentically possess or replicate.

Moreover, ethical decision-making presents a gap. AI's logic is bound by its programming and datasets; it lacks the moral conscience to weigh decisions' ethical implications as humans can. This limitation is critical in situations requiring moral judgments that consider societal norms and values, highlighting the indispensable role of human oversight in AI's application.

As we continue to explore AI's capabilities, these gaps underscore the importance of fostering a synergy between human creativity, empathy, and technology, ensuring that AI enhances rather than attempts to replace the uniquely human aspects of our existence.

# 4.
# SILICON EMPATHY IN ACTION

> "Humans are limited in the attention, kindness and compassion that they can expend to others, but AI based compassionate robots can channel virtually unlimited resources into building compassionate relationships in the society."
>
> **Amit Ray, Compassionate Artificial Intelligence: Frameworks and Algorithms**

A common trait among the industry giants discussed in this book is their unyielding drive for innovation and change. Regardless of whether they've been in the market for a decade or a century, these companies understand that stagnation is not an option. Their willingness to evolve and adopt emerging technologies has been crucial to their success.

A prime example of this adaptability is Teleperformance, which has grown to become the largest BPO company globally, boasting nearly 500,000 employees across over 95 countries. However, Teleperformance's journey began modestly in Paris 45 years ago with just Daniel Julien and 12 phone lines. Julien's openness to change has been a key factor in the company's growth.

From incorporating email shortly after the internet's public emergence to later integrating chat, social media, and trust & safety services, Teleperformance has consistently embraced new technologies. Today, the company views AI and other emerging technologies not as threats, but as golden opportunities to further enhance their services and reach.

# BLUEPRINT TO CHANGE

The framework depicted here illustrates the intricate relationship between vision, skills, incentive, resources, and action plans as key drivers of change within an organization or system. When these elements are balanced and effectively aligned, they foster an environment conducive to change, promoting growth and innovation. However, the absence of any one element can lead to negative feelings or states such as confusion, anxiety, resistance, frustration, or a sense of running in place without progress. This framework serves as a blueprint for leaders and change agents to understand the necessary components for successful transformation and to diagnose potential issues that could hinder the change process.

# THE FRAMEWORK TO CHANGE...

| VISION | SKILLS | INCENTIVE | RESOURCE | ACTION PAN | = CHANGE |
|--------|--------|-----------|----------|------------|----------|
| VISION | SKILLS | INCENTIVE | RESOURCE | ACTION PAN | = CONFUSION |
| VISION | SKILLS | INCENTIVE | RESOURCE | ACTION PAN | = ANXIETY |
| VISION | SKILLS | INCENTIVE | RESOURCE | ACTION PAN | = RESISTANCE |
| VISION | SKILLS | INCENTIVE | RESOURCE | ACTION PAN | = FRUSTRATION |
| VISION | SKILLS | INCENTIVE | RESOURCE | ACTION PAN | = TREADMILL |

# CASE STUDIES FROM INDUSTRY GIANTS

"Silicon Empathy in Action" showcases how empathy and AI integration are being applied by industry giants to revolutionize customer experience, operational efficiency, and innovation. This section will explore case studies from companies like leaders in automotive industry, Google, and Microsoft, illustrating their pioneering work in embedding empathy into AI technologies. Through initiatives like Google's AI for Social Good and Microsoft's AI-driven accessibility tools, these corporations demonstrate the profound impact of Silicon Empathy. These examples not only highlight the technological feats achieved but also underscore the importance of centering human empathy in AI development, paving the way for a future where technology enhances, rather than detracts from, the human experience.

# GERMAN-BASED AUTOMOTIVE LEADER

In an innovative venture outside of Germany, a European contact center tasked with written customer support for a prominent German automotive maker encountered challenges with average handle time (AHT) and customer satisfaction (CSAT). This case, one of the first AI projects I contributed to, involved a deep dive into the customer journey and a comprehensive Lean Six Sigma analysis to pinpoint underlying issues. We identified two primary obstacles: the considerable time required for agents to draft original emails and the complexity of writing in grammatically accurate German.

The solution was the implementation of a generative AI tool adept at summarizing and crafting new emails, perfectly aligned with the customer's intent and tone, yet original in context and impeccably written in German. This intervention led to a remarkable 20% reduction in AHT and a leap in CSAT from about 60% to over 80%, effectively eliminating customer complaints about language proficiency. This story exemplifies the essence of Silicon Empathy, demonstrating AI's capability to transcend linguistic barriers and significantly enhance the quality of customer interaction.

# GOOGLE: AI FOR SOCIAL GOOD

Google's AI for Social Good initiative leverages AI to tackle some of the world's most significant challenges. By applying machine learning to problems in health, crisis response, and environmental conservation, Google demonstrates how AI can be used empathetically to benefit society. For example, their flood forecasting system helps warn communities of impending floods, potentially saving lives through advanced prediction and alert systems.

# MICROSOFT: AI-DRIVEN ACCESSIBILITY TOOLS

Microsoft's commitment to making technology accessible to everyone has led to the development of AI-driven tools designed to assist people with disabilities. The Seeing AI app, for instance, provides a remarkable example of how technology can be used empathetically to enhance the lives of visually impaired users, narrating the world around them and thus making daily tasks more manageable.

Launched on July 12, 2017, for iOS devices, Seeing AI harnesses the power of artificial intelligence to bridge the gap between technology and human needs. Through the simple use of a device's camera, the application identifies people and objects in the environment and conveys this information audibly to users with visual impairments. Available in 16 languages, Seeing AI exemplifies how AI can be leveraged to create more inclusive and empathetic technological solutions, truly reflecting the essence of Silicon Empathy in action.

Through these case studies, it becomes evident that when industry giants harness AI with a focus on empathy, technology transcends its traditional boundaries, becoming a powerful agent of positive change and a catalyst for more inclusive, compassionate, and human-centered experiences.

# SMALL BUSINESSES AND STARTUPS: A NEW FRONTIER

In the realm of small businesses and startups, AI has heralded a new frontier of innovation and efficiency. The advent of AI technologies has democratized access to advanced tools, enabling even the smallest entities to leverage data analytics, automate processes, and enhance customer experiences. Notably, the trend towards AI integration has coincided with a significant increase in startup formations, as entrepreneurs leverage AI to create solutions that address niche markets and complex problems with greater precision and scalability. This surge reflects a broader shift in the business landscape, where AI capabilities are increasingly seen as essential to competitiveness and growth in the digital age.

Small companies and AI startups stand at the forefront of innovation, often focusing on specific demographics and developing specialized solutions that larger corporations may overlook. These entities are agile, able to quickly adapt to new technologies and market demands, making them integral to the rapid evolution of AI applications across industries. Their growth reflects a broader trend towards digital transformation, emphasizing the critical role of AI in shaping future business strategies and economic landscapes.

The statistical growth highlighted by reputable sources underscores a pivotal shift in the business landscape, driven by AI.

eWeek's[1] observation that the number of US AI companies has more than doubled since 2017 illustrates the rapid embrace of AI within the entrepreneurial sector. This growth is not confined to the US; IBM's findings show an even more aggressive adoption in markets like China and India, surpassing the global average significantly. Such trends underscore the global appeal of AI technologies among startups, keen on leveraging AI for competitive advantage.

Stanford University's report on AI funding magnifies the financial commitment to AI innovation, with a staggering increase that reached $93.5 billion in 2021. This influx of investment fuels the development of AI applications, from analytics to customer service enhancements, empowering startups to scale and innovate at an unprecedented pace.

Next Move Strategy Consulting's projection that global AI revenue will exceed $1.8 trillion by 2030 further highlights the economic significance of AI. This anticipated growth reflects the vast potential for AI to redefine business models, streamline operations, and open new markets.

These statistics not only illustrate the growing integration of AI in the startup ecosystem but also predict a future where AI's influence continues to expand, shaping a new era of innovation and entrepreneurship. As startups and small businesses increasingly adopt AI, they not only contribute to this growth but also benefit from the enhanced capabilities AI offers, from operational efficiency to new product and service

---

[1] eWeek formerly PCWeek, is a technology and business magazine.

innovation, marking a transformative period in the global business narrative.

# THE FOUNDER'S PERSPECTIVE

When I embarked on the journey of writing this book, I had the privilege of engaging in deep conversations with Oleh Kurtianyk, a visionary tech entrepreneur, startup founder, and esteemed member of the Forbes Tech Council. Our discussions wandered through the vast landscape of AI, during which Oleh imparted a uniquely fresh and compelling perspective that resonated deeply with me. He articulated a thought-provoking analogy: Throughout history, and likely even before recorded times, humanity has consistently sought external aids to simplify life and achieve tasks more efficiently. Just as early humans didn't rely on bare hands for hunting but instead innovated with tools like sticks and stones, and later, more sophisticated weapons, to secure food more effectively, we now harness AI to streamline our lives and tackle complex challenges. This analogy underscored AI's role as the modern tool in our continuous quest to enhance human capability and ease, marking a profound moment of insight that enriched the foundations of this book.

Oleh further expanded our dialogue with analogies highlighting the evolution of automation. He pointed out that our journey with automation didn't begin with the modern conveniences of RPAs (Robotic Process Automation) and RDAs (Robotic Desktop Automation) on computers. Historically, we automated essential tasks and even entire jobs through the use of animals, such as horses and oxen, which served as our initial 'tools' for easing laborious work. This practice of leveraging external forces for automation saw a significant shift in the 19th century with the advent of steam engines, marking a pivotal moment in human ingenuity and our relentless pursuit of efficiency. This historical perspective provided by Oleh not only enriched our discussions but also offered a profound understanding of the continuum in which AI automation exists today, as the latest chapter in humanity's ongoing narrative of innovation.

Oleh also shared an insightful comparison that strikingly illustrates AI's role in modern technology: likening AI to calculators but for text. This analogy helps demystify AI, presenting it as a "text calculator" that performs operations on text with remarkable speed, akin to how calculators simplify numerical tasks. This perspective not only makes AI more accessible but also underscores its utility in enhancing human productivity and creativity by handling complex text-based operations efficiently.

Furthermore, his latest venture, unwink.ai, embodies the practical application of our shared beliefs in Silicon Empathy. Unwink.ai is an innovative AI model designed to measure, organize, and categorize data, while also automatically generating clear insights and creating actionable tickets. This tool exemplifies how AI, when developed with empathy and an understanding of human needs, can transform data into meaningful action, further reinforcing our vision of AI as a powerful ally in the pursuit of knowledge and efficiency.

In the culmination of our discussions, It became abundantly clear that Oleh and I share a fundamental alignment in our values and beliefs, particularly in our advocacy for the Silicon Empathy concept. As loyal advocates of this philosophy, we believe deeply in the potential of AI as a formidable tool for human advancement, provided it is wielded with an empathy-first approach. Our conversations solidified our mutual conviction that AI, when guided by empathy, holds the power to empower individuals and societies rather than replacing them. This shared vision for a future where technology enhances human capability and connection forms the cornerstone of our discussions and the essence of this book's message.

# THE ROLE OF AI IN ENHANCING CUSTOMER EXPERIENCE

The advent of AI in enhancing customer experience (CX) is transforming the landscape of business-customer interactions. Central to this transformation is the power of AI in personalization, data analysis, and intelligent automation. Through personalization, businesses can offer tailored experiences, meeting customers' expectations for relevance and convenience. Data analysis enables a deeper understanding of customer behaviors and preferences, informing strategies that anticipate needs. Intelligent Automation, particularly through Robotic Process Automation (RPA), streamlines operations, ensuring efficient service delivery. This synergy of AI-driven capabilities fosters a CX that is not only seamless but also deeply resonant with individual customer desires, setting a new benchmark for customer engagement and satisfaction.

At the intersection of AI and customer experience, we witness the transformative power of technology guided by Silicon Empathy. Central to this revolution are personalization, data analysis, and intelligent automation, elements that together enhance the customer journey in unprecedented ways.

## PERSONALIZATION AND HYPER-PERSONALIZATION

AI's ability to offer personalization, or even hyper-personalization, stands as a testament to its impact. By analyzing customer data, AI enables businesses to tailor experiences, recommendations, and communications uniquely suited to individual preferences. This level of customization not only elevates customer satisfaction but also fosters loyalty, as consumers are more likely to engage with services that resonate with their personal needs and interests.

AI analyzes customer data, such as past purchases, browsing behavior, and preferences, to offer personalized recommendations, content, and services. This tailored approach increases engagement and satisfaction by making customers feel understood and valued. For example, in e-commerce, AI can provide real-time support and information during the customer journey. It can suggest complementary products during checkout or offer instant help through chatbots when a customer appears stuck on a page.

# DATA ANALYSIS: THE BACKBONE OF INFORMED DECISIONS

Through meticulous data analysis, AI uncovers patterns and insights hidden within vast amounts of information. This capability allows businesses to understand customer behaviors, predict trends, and make informed decisions that align with consumer desires. By leveraging AI for deep analysis, companies can craft strategies that are both effective and empathetic, ensuring that every decision contributes to a positive customer experience.

AI tools can predict customer behavior, such as potential churn or the likelihood of a purchase, based on historical data. Businesses can use these insights to proactively address concerns, tailor marketing strategies, and improve retention rates.

# INTELLIGENT AUTOMATION THROUGH RPA

Robotic Process Automation (RPA) exemplifies intelligent automation, streamlining business processes and customer interactions with precision and efficiency. RPA tools, powered by AI, automate repetitive tasks, freeing human agents to focus on areas requiring human empathy and creativity. This not only boosts operational efficiency but also enhances the quality of customer service, providing quick and accurate responses to inquiries and improving overall customer engagement.

By automating routine tasks and optimizing operations, AI reduces wait times, improves accuracy, and cuts costs. These savings can be passed on to customers in the form of lower prices or better services.

These components—personalization, data analysis, and intelligent automation—demonstrate AI's crucial role in redefining customer experiences. By integrating these AI-driven approaches, businesses can create more meaningful, efficient, and satisfying interactions, showcasing the true potential of Silicon Empathy in action.

# 5.
# THE ETHICAL DIMENSIONS OF AI

"By far the greatest danger of Artificial Intelligence is that people conclude too early that they understand it."

**Eliezer Yudkowsky**

# NAVIGATING THE MORAL MAZE

The ethical dimensions of AI involve navigating a complex moral landscape, where technology's potential for societal benefit is weighed against concerns of privacy, bias, and autonomy. As AI systems become more integrated into everyday life, ethical considerations must guide their development and deployment. This includes ensuring AI operates transparently, respects user privacy, and is designed free of biases that could lead to unfair outcomes. Ethical AI also requires accountability mechanisms, where decisions made by AI systems can be explained and challenged. This chapter delves into the moral intricacies AI presents, exploring how developers, policymakers, and society can work together to ensure AI serves the greater good while minimizing potential harms.

To navigate the moral maze of AI, we begin by defining ethical AI as technology developed and used in a way that is transparent, fair, and respects both privacy and human rights.

This involves developers creating unbiased algorithms, policymakers enacting regulations that ensure AI's benefits are widely distributed and do not harm societal values, and society at large staying informed and engaged in discussions about AI's role and impact. Collaboration across these groups is essential to address the ethical challenges AI presents, ensuring technology advances in a manner that benefits humanity while safeguarding against potential misuses.

By examining real-world scenarios and emerging discussions around data ownership, transparency in AI algorithms, and the need for human-centric design principles, I aim to highlight the importance of developing AI responsibly. I put accent on ethical frameworks, public engagement, and international collaboration as essential steps towards fostering ethical AI development and deployment, ensuring technology advances align with societal values and contribute positively to human well-being.

As artificial intelligence (AI) weaves its way more deeply into the fabric of our lives, it brings not only unprecedented advancements but also complex ethical dilemmas. These challenges require us to carefully consider the implications of AI's integration into healthcare, finance, transportation, and beyond.  Should AI be allowed to make life-altering decisions without human oversight? How can we ensure AI does not exacerbate social inequalities? What is the appropriate balance between leveraging AI for surveillance and protecting individual privacy? These are all important dilemmas being discussed over and over again between policymakers, developers and promotors of AI.

At the heart of AI's ethical considerations is the data that fuels it. The collection, use, and storage of vast amounts of personal information pose significant privacy and security risks. Ensuring the balance between leveraging data for AI's advancements and protecting individuals' privacy rights is a pivotal concern. As AI systems are trained on this data, the potential for algorithmic bias emerges, where prejudices present in the data can lead to discriminatory outcomes. This necessitates a commitment to developing AI with diverse datasets and rigorous testing to mitigate biases.

Moreover, the questions of data ownership and control are paramount. As individuals increasingly become the source of data powering AI, establishing frameworks that allow for meaningful consent and control over personal information is essential.

Beyond the data and algorithms, the human element in AI development cannot be overlooked. The responsibility for ethical AI deployment lies with a broad spectrum of stakeholders, including engineers, policymakers, and the broader society. Transparency and explainability in AI systems are crucial for building trust and ensuring accountability. Clear lines of responsibility must be established to address and rectify any harm caused by AI systems.

To navigate this moral maze, a multi-faceted approach is necessary. Developing robust ethical frameworks, engaging the public in informed discussions about AI, and fostering international collaboration on ethical standards are critical steps forward. Continuous learning and adaptation to the evolving AI landscape will ensure that ethical considerations remain at the forefront of technological advancement.

In charting a course for ethical AI, we are tasked with not only harnessing its potential for good but also vigilantly guarding against its potential harms. By prioritizing human values and ethical principles in the development and deployment of AI, we can navigate the complexities of this new frontier and realize a future where technology enhances human dignity, equity, and the collective well-being.

# NEW CAR SOLD FOR 1$

In a notable incident highlighting the ethical challenges of AI in real-world applications, a GM[1] dealership's chatbot was manipulated into "agreeing" to sell a Chevy Tahoe, valued at over $76,000, for merely $1. This event unfolded when Chris White, a musician and software engineer, explored the limits of the dealership's AI chatbot, powered by ChatGPT. His experimentation led to another individual, Chris Bakke, exploiting the chatbot's programming to secure a "legally binding" deal for the Tahoe at an absurdly low price. The dealership, caught off guard by the chatbot's vulnerability, subsequently disabled the AI feature. This incident serves as a stark reminder of the importance of ethical considerations, thorough testing, and the need for human oversight in deploying AI technologies to prevent misuse and ensure they align with intended ethical and operational guidelines.

# PRIVACY, SECURITY, AND TRUST IN AN AI-DRIVEN WORLD

In an AI-driven world, privacy, security, and trust form the cornerstone of ethical AI deployment. As AI systems increasingly handle sensitive personal and corporate data, ensuring these technologies respect user privacy and are secure against breaches is paramount. Trust in AI also hinges

---

[1] General Motors Company is an American multinational automotive manufacturing company headquartered in Detroit, Michigan, United States. The company is most known for owning and manufacturing four automobile brands, Chevrolet, GMC, Cadillac and Buick.

on transparency and accountability, where users understand how AI systems make decisions. Ahead we explore the challenges and solutions in building AI systems that safeguard privacy, enhance security, and maintain the trust of users, emphasizing the need for robust ethical frameworks and continuous dialogue between technology developers, policymakers, and the public to navigate these critical issues[1].

As AI becomes increasingly integrated into our daily lives, the issues of privacy, security, and trust emerge as critical ethical considerations. Ensuring the confidentiality of personal data processed by AI, safeguarding against breaches, and maintaining the integrity of AI systems are paramount for fostering trust between technology and its users. We delve into the complexities of protecting privacy in an era where data is a valuable commodity, highlights the challenges of securing AI systems from potential threats, and discuss the importance of building trust through transparency and accountability in AI operations. Through real-world examples and proposed solutions, we explore how developers, policymakers, and society can collaborate to address these concerns, ensuring AI advances in a manner that respects individual rights and promotes security.

In the digital age, the advent of artificial intelligence has ushered in a new era of possibilities, transforming every facet of our lives. Yet, this transformation brings to the forefront the critical issues of privacy, security, and trust—elements that are foundational to the ethical deployment and acceptance of AI technologies. As we navigate through the complexities of an AI-driven world, the balance between leveraging the benefits of AI and safeguarding individual rights becomes paramount.

---

[1] The AI Act is a proposed EU law on artificial intelligence (AI) – the first comprehensive law on AI by a major regulator anywhere. The Act is akin to Europe's GDPR, passed in 2016, but for AI. It imposes requirements on companies designing and/or using AI in the EU, and backs it up with stiff penalties.

# PRIVACY: THE CORNERSTONE OF DIGITAL TRUST

Privacy concerns in AI span from the collection and use of personal data to its storage and potential misuse. Ensuring data privacy means not only protecting personal information from unauthorized access but also empowering individuals with control over their data. It involves transparent policies and practices that respect user consent, providing a clear understanding of how data is used to train AI systems.

Privacy in AI is a critical issue that revolves around how personal data is collected, used, and protected by AI systems. Ensuring privacy involves implementing robust data protection measures, such as encryption and anonymization, to safeguard personal information from unauthorized access and potential misuse. It also requires transparent data practices that respect user consent, providing individuals with control over their data. Addressing privacy in AI is essential for maintaining user trust and ensuring the ethical deployment of AI technologies.

# SECURITY: SAFEGUARDING THE FUTURE

The security of AI systems is vital in preventing data breaches and cyber attacks that could compromise personal information or the integrity of critical infrastructure. Implementing robust security measures, such as advanced encryption techniques and continuous monitoring for vulnerabilities, ensures the integrity and reliability of AI applications, building a foundation of trust with users.

Security in AI encompasses protecting data and systems from unauthorized access and cyber threats. It's crucial for companies to implement strong security measures to safeguard sensitive information. This involves using advanced encryption, conducting regular security audits, and adopting secure data practices. Ensuring data security is fundamental to maintaining trust with users and is a key responsibility of companies deploying AI technologies. Effective security protocols not only protect data integrity but also reinforce the company's commitment to ethical AI use.

# TRUST: BUILDING CONFIDENCE IN AI

Trust in AI is cultivated through transparency and accountability. Users need to understand how AI systems make decisions to trust their outputs. Efforts to make AI systems more explainable and decisions more interpretable are crucial in building this trust. Furthermore, establishing clear accountability for AI decisions ensures that there are mechanisms in place to address any issues or harms that arise, reinforcing public confidence in AI technologies.

The statistic that 62% of consumers are willing to submit data to AI for better experiences with businesses highlights the significant trust placed in AI technologies. This trust is foundational for the successful integration of AI into various services, emphasizing the importance of companies in maintaining ethical standards, transparent practices, and robust security measures to protect consumer data. Trust in AI not only fosters greater user engagement but also encourages the responsible and beneficial use of technology in enhancing customer experiences.

# NAVIGATING THE PATH FORWARD

The journey towards achieving privacy, security, and trust in AI involves a collaborative effort among developers, policymakers, and the public. Developing ethical frameworks and guidelines, engaging in open dialogue about AI's impact, and fostering international cooperation are essential steps in navigating the moral maze of AI. By prioritizing these ethical considerations, we pave the way for a future where AI technologies not only advance human progress but also uphold our shared values and rights.

# THE RESPONSIBILITY OF CREATORS

In the evolving landscape of artificial intelligence, the responsibility of creators emerges as a foundational pillar. This duty extends beyond the technical development of AI systems to encompass a deep commitment to ethical principles. As architects of the digital future, creators hold the power to shape how AI influences society, making it imperative that they prioritize the well-being of individuals and the collective.

# ETHICAL FOUNDATIONS AND SOCIETAL IMPACT

Creators are tasked with embedding ethical considerations into the very fabric of AI technologies. This includes ensuring fairness, preventing bias, and designing with privacy and security at the forefront. The societal impact of AI is profound, and as such, creators must navigate the ethical implications of their work with diligence and foresight.

The ethical foundations of AI focus on ensuring technology development adheres to principles of fairness, accountability, and transparency. This ethical grounding aims to prevent biases in AI algorithms that could lead to discriminatory outcomes, safeguarding against potential societal harms. The societal impact of AI is significant, offering the potential to enhance healthcare, education, and economic opportunities, but also posing risks related to privacy, employment, and social inequality. Creators bear the responsibility to weigh these factors, striving to maximize benefits while minimizing harms, ensuring AI serves as a force for good in society.

# TRANSPARENCY AND EXPLAINABILITY

A key aspect of creators' responsibility is fostering transparency in AI systems. This involves making AI's decision-making processes understandable and accessible to users and stakeholders, ensuring that technology remains a tool for empowerment rather than obscurity.

Transparency and explainability in AI are crucial for building trust and ensuring accountability. They involve making the inner workings of AI systems clear to users and stakeholders, enabling them to understand how decisions are made. This clarity is essential for evaluating the fairness and accuracy of AI, facilitating informed consent, and enabling recourse if biases or errors occur. Creators must strive to develop AI systems whose processes and outcomes can be easily interpreted, ensuring that AI acts as an empowering tool rather than an opaque, unaccountable force in society.

# ONGOING VIGILANCE AND ADAPTATION

The dynamic nature of AI requires creators to adopt a stance of ongoing vigilance, continually assessing and addressing potential biases or harms that may arise. This proactive approach ensures that AI systems evolve in alignment with ethical standards and societal values.

The rapid evolution of AI necessitates ongoing vigilance and adaptation by creators to ensure ethical standards are maintained. This involves continuously monitoring AI systems for unintended consequences, biases, or ethical lapses and adapting these systems in response to new insights and societal changes. Vigilance ensures that AI technologies remain aligned with ethical principles over time, while adaptation allows for the incorporation of advancements in ethical understanding and AI capabilities, ensuring that AI systems are both effective and ethically sound in their applications.

# COLLABORATION AND DIALOGUE

Finally, the responsibility of creators encompasses engaging in open dialogue with policymakers, industry peers, and the broader public. By fostering a collaborative environment, creators can contribute to the development of robust ethical frameworks and guidelines that guide the responsible advancement of AI.

Collaboration and dialogue are essential for the ethical development and implementation of AI. This involves creators engaging with policymakers, industry peers, and the broader public to share knowledge, discuss ethical considerations, and develop consensus on best practices. Through open dialogue, diverse perspectives can inform AI development, ensuring technologies are inclusive and equitable. Collaboration fosters the creation of comprehensive ethical frameworks and standards that guide AI use, ensuring it aligns with societal values and contributes positively to human well-being.

In embracing these responsibilities, creators not only contribute to the ethical development of AI but also help forge a future where technology aligns with humanity's highest ideals, enhancing lives while safeguarding dignity and rights.

Bill Gates shared his awe at witnessing AI's capabilities during a visit to OpenAI, where he challenged the team to train an AI model, GPT, to pass an Advanced Placement biology exam. Expecting the challenge to take years, Gates was astounded when the AI accomplished it in months, achieving the highest score. This experience, highlighted in his March 21, 2023, article, underscores the rapid advancements in AI, echoing the transformative potential Gates saw in early computing innovations. Gates envisions AI reshaping work, health, education, and addressing global inequities, emphasizing the need for ethical development and application to ensure benefits are universally accessible.

# 6.
# BUILDING A BRIDGE BETWEEN AI AND HUMANITY

"As more and more artificial intelligence is entering into the world, more and more emotional intelligence must enter into leadership."

**Amit Ray**

## DESIGNING WITH EMPATHY: PRINCIPLES AND PRACTICES

By designing with empathy a bridge between AI and Humanity, I envision integrating empathetic principles into AI development to ensure technologies align with human values and needs. It involves understanding and addressing the diverse impacts of AI on society, ensuring inclusivity, and prioritizing user well-being. I continuously advocate for a human-centered approach to AI design, focusing on collaboration between technologists, ethicists, and end-users to create AI solutions that enhance, rather than diminish, the human experience. Through practical examples and guidelines, it outlines how to embed empathy into AI, fostering technologies that truly serve humanity.

To craft the sub-chapter "Designing with Empathy: Principles and Practices," I am focusing on creating AI with a deep understanding of and compassion for human needs and experiences. This approach involves actively considering the emotional and societal impacts of AI technologies, ensuring they support and enhance human well-being. Incorporating empathy into the design process—termed "empathy embedded for success"—ensures AI solutions are not only technically proficient but also genuinely beneficial and accessible to all segments of society. This method emphasizes the importance of multidisciplinary collaboration, involving ethicists, psychologists, and end-users in AI development to create technologies that respect and understand the diversity of human conditions and aspirations.

In the journey towards harmonizing AI with human needs, "Designing with Empathy: Principles and Practices" emerges as a crucial guidepost. This philosophy, encapsulated by the mantra "empathy embedded for success," advocates for a development process where understanding and addressing human emotions and societal impacts are paramount. Empathetic design in AI doesn't merely aim to create technology that is functional but seeks to forge connections that are meaningful and enriching.

# FOUNDATIONAL PRINCIPLES

At the heart of empathetic AI design are foundational principles that prioritize the human experience. This involves recognizing the diversity of human conditions and ensuring AI systems are accessible, inclusive, and supportive of all users. By embedding empathy from the outset, developers can anticipate and mitigate potential negative impacts, aligning technology's evolution with ethical imperatives.

The foundational principles of designing AI with empathy focus on ensuring technologies are developed with a deep understanding of and commitment to human values. This includes prioritizing inclusivity, ensuring accessibility for all users regardless of their background or abilities, and designing with privacy and ethical considerations at the forefront. It's about recognizing the diverse experiences of individuals and striving to create AI solutions that respect and enhance human dignity and rights. These principles act as a moral compass for developers, guiding the creation of AI technologies that are not only innovative but also equitable and supportive of human well-being.

## COLLABORATIVE PRACTICES

The practice of designing empathetic AI is inherently collaborative, requiring input from ethicists, sociologists, psychologists, and the end-users themselves. Such multidisciplinary collaboration ensures a broad spectrum of human experiences and needs are considered, making AI systems more adaptable and responsive to the nuances of human life.

Collaborative practices in AI design involve multidisciplinary teams working together to infuse empathy into technology. This process brings together AI developers, ethicists, user experience designers, and the end-users themselves to ensure a holistic understanding of human needs. By incorporating diverse perspectives, AI can be developed to serve a wide range of societal roles effectively, ensuring the technology is inclusive, equitable, and capable of addressing real-world challenges with sensitivity and understanding. Collaboration ensures AI solutions are not only technically sound but also ethically aligned and human-centric.

## EMPATHY IN ACTION

Implementing empathy in AI design also means continuously engaging with and learning from the communities affected by these technologies. This iterative process allows for the refinement of AI systems in response to evolving societal values and needs, ensuring technology remains a positive force in users' lives.

"Empathy in Action" in AI design means translating empathetic principles into tangible outcomes by actively engaging with and learning from the communities affected by AI technologies. This involves iterative design processes where feedback from end-users is continuously sought and incorporated, ensuring AI solutions remain aligned with human values and needs over time. By doing so, AI developers can create systems that genuinely support and enhance the human experience, demonstrating a commitment to using technology as a force for good in society.

# ETHICAL AND PRACTICAL OUTCOMES

With "empathy embedded for success," the outcome is twofold: ethically aligned technologies that respect and enhance human dignity, and practical solutions that address real-world challenges in innovative and compassionate ways. This approach not only elevates the potential of AI to benefit humanity but also builds a foundation of trust and reliability between technology and society.

Incorporating empathy into AI design leads to ethical and practical outcomes that significantly impact society. Ethically, it ensures AI technologies are developed with a commitment to fairness, privacy, and inclusivity, respecting human dignity. Practically, empathetic AI can provide solutions that are deeply aligned with human needs, enhancing areas such as healthcare, education, and accessibility. This dual focus not only advances technology but also fosters a more equitable and understanding world, demonstrating the profound potential of AI when guided by empathy.

By adhering to these principles and practices, "Designing with Empathy" sets a path for developing AI that truly understands and serves humanity, bridging the gap between technological innovation and the fundamental human need for connection and understanding.

# ENCOURAGING EMOTIONAL INTELLIGENCE IN AI DEVELOPMENT

Emotional intelligence embodies the capacity to comprehend, manage, and articulate one's own feelings, as well as interpret and respond to the emotions of others. It includes recognizing and naming our emotions, harnessing these feelings to guide thinking and actions, regulating emotions within ourselves, and influencing others' emotional states in positive ways. This skill set is crucial for personal well-being and effective interpersonal relations, enabling us to navigate the complexities of social interactions with empathy and understanding.

It's important to put accent on on integrating the capacity for empathy, social skills, and emotional understanding into AI systems. This involves programming AI to recognize and respond appropriately to human emotions, enhancing interactions between humans and machines. By incorporating emotional intelligence, AI can better serve and support users in a variety of contexts, from customer service to mental health support, making technology more relatable and effective in meeting human needs. We explore strategies and technologies enabling AI to understand and engage with the emotional dynamics of human interactions.

In "Encouraging Emotional Intelligence in AI Development," the focus shifts to embedding AI with the ability to understand, interpret, and respond to human emotions, a key aspect of creating more intuitive and human-centric technologies. This endeavor involves leveraging advances in natural language processing, facial recognition, and sentiment analysis to enable AI systems to discern and adapt to the emotional states of users. By prioritizing emotional intelligence, AI developers can enhance the usability and effectiveness of AI applications across various domains, from healthcare to customer service, fostering technologies that not only think but also feel in alignment with human needs and emotions.

# ENCOURAGING EMOTIONAL INTELLIGENCE IN AI DEVELOPMENT

The quest to imbue AI with emotional intelligence is a transformative step towards forging deeper connections between technology and humanity, delving into the pivotal role emotional intelligence plays in AI development, aiming to create systems that not only process information but also understand and respond to human emotions effectively.

Emotional intelligence in AI encompasses the technology's ability to recognize, interpret, and react to human emotions, enabling AI to engage in more meaningful and supportive interactions. This capability is crucial across various sectors, enhancing customer service with AI that can detect and adapt to a customer's mood, providing empathetic support in mental health applications, and creating educational tools that respond to the emotional state of learners.

To achieve this, developers integrate advanced machine learning algorithms, natural language processing, and emotional recognition technologies into AI systems. These tools allow AI to analyze verbal cues, facial expressions, and other forms of non-verbal communication, giving it a nuanced understanding of human emotions.

However, developing emotionally intelligent AI also presents ethical challenges, necessitating careful consideration of privacy and the potential impact on users. It requires a collaborative approach, engaging ethicists, psychologists, and end-users in the development process, ensuring AI systems are designed with empathy and respect for human dignity.

By championing emotional intelligence in AI, we pave the way for technologies that not only enhance efficiency but also enrich the human experience, offering support and understanding in an increasingly digital world. This journey towards emotionally intelligent AI represents a crucial evolution in technology, one that holds the promise of building a bridge between AI and humanity through empathy embedded for success.

# THE IMPORTANCE OF KEEPING HUMANS IN THE LOOP

Human oversight and interaction in the AI systems play a critical role. This approach ensures AI decisions and actions remain aligned with ethical standards and societal values. Human involvement is crucial for interpreting complex or ambiguous situations, providing empathy and understanding that AI currently lacks, and making adjustments to AI systems based on evolving contexts and needs. It highlights strategies for effectively integrating human judgment with AI capabilities, ensuring technology serves humanity's best interests and fostering trust in AI applications.

This ensures AI operates within ethical bounds and aligns with societal norms. It stresses human judgment's role in interpreting nuanced scenarios AI might misread, providing the essential human touch AI lacks. Exploring methods to integrate human insights with AI efficiency, advocating for a balanced partnership where technology amplifies human capabilities while being steered by human values and ethics, fostering a symbiotic relationship between AI advancements and human oversight.

It advocates for a symbiotic relationship where AI enhances human decision-making without replacing it. It ensures AI applications are guided by human judgment, especially in complex, nuanced scenarios where empathy and moral considerations are paramount. I am, day after day, and night after night, exploring strategies to maintain this vital human-AI collaboration, ensuring technology remains an empowering tool that upholds and enriches the human experience.

In an era where artificial intelligence is becoming increasingly integrated into every aspect of our lives, "The Importance of Keeping Humans in the Loop" emerges as a crucial paradigm. This principle advocates for a harmonious blend of human intuition and AI's computational power, ensuring that AI systems are not only efficient but also aligned with ethical standards and societal expectations.

# HUMAN OVERSIGHT: A PILLAR OF ETHICAL AI

At the core of maintaining human oversight is the belief that, despite AI's advanced capabilities, the human perspective remains irreplaceable, especially in making nuanced decisions that require empathy, moral judgment, and understanding of complex social contexts. This approach prevents AI from operating in a vacuum, ensuring its actions are continually guided by human values.

Human oversight in AI development is pivotal for ensuring technology aligns with ethical standards and societal norms. This oversight involves constant human engagement in AI's decision-making processes, guaranteeing that AI operations consider ethical complexities, cultural sensitivities, and moral implications beyond raw data analysis. It serves as a safeguard against biases and ensures AI systems are developed and deployed responsibly. Through human oversight, AI's potential is harnessed to complement human judgment, fostering technology that respects human dignity and promotes fairness and inclusivity in its applications.

# COLLABORATIVE INTELLIGENCE: ENHANCING DECISION-MAKING

The concept of collaborative intelligence underlines the synergy between human creativity and AI's analytical prowess. By keeping humans in the loop, AI becomes a tool that amplifies human capabilities rather than replacing them, fostering an environment where technology serves to enhance the richness of human experience.

Collaborative intelligence between humans and AI enhances decision-making by combining human emotional intelligence and AI's data-processing capabilities. This partnership allows for nuanced decisions that consider ethical implications, cultural context, and individual human needs. By leveraging the strengths of both human judgment and AI analysis, collaborative intelligence ensures more balanced, fair, and effective outcomes in various applications, from healthcare to customer service, making AI a powerful ally in solving complex problems and making informed decisions.

# ADAPTABILITY AND LEARNING: THE HUMAN-AI FEEDBACK LOOP

Incorporating human feedback into AI development is vital for its adaptability and learning. This feedback loop allows AI systems to evolve based on real-world experiences and changing societal norms, ensuring technology remains relevant and beneficial across different contexts and times.

The Human-AI Feedback Loop is essential for adaptability and learning in AI systems. It enables continuous improvement through real-world interactions and human feedback, ensuring AI remains relevant and effective over time. This process fosters AI's ability to learn from diverse situations and evolve, enhancing its utility and ensuring it meets the changing needs and values of society. Through this feedback loop, AI can adjust its algorithms, reducing biases and inaccuracies, and better serve its intended purpose, demonstrating a dynamic approach to AI development and deployment.

# BUILDING TRUST THROUGH TRANSPARENCY

Keeping humans in the loop also plays a critical role in building trust in AI technologies. When users understand that human judgment is a key component of AI systems, it reassures them that technology is being used responsibly, enhancing their confidence in AI applications.

Building trust through transparency in AI involves clear communication about how AI systems operate and make decisions. This transparency reassures users and stakeholders that AI is being used ethically and responsibly.

It's about demystifying AI processes, allowing for accountability and fostering confidence in AI applications. When people understand the rationale behind AI's actions, it builds trust, ensuring the technology is viewed as a reliable and beneficial tool, integral to achieving ethical AI deployment and acceptance in society.

# HUMAN OVERSIGHT IN AVIATION

Historically, the aviation industry showcases the importance of keeping humans in the loop. For instance, advanced autopilot systems in aircraft[1] are designed to handle a wide range of flying tasks, yet pilots are always present to oversee these systems. This human oversight ensures that, in unexpected situations or emergencies, human judgment and experience can intervene, making critical decisions that AI alone might not be equipped to handle. This balance between technology and human expertise exemplifies the critical role of human oversight in complex systems.

---

[1] The first aircraft autopilot was developed by Sperry Corp. in 1912 and it was designed to perform some basic pilot tasks.

# 7.
## THE FUTURE IS NOW

"Even a cat has things it can do that AI cannot."

**Fei-Fei Li**

# EMERGING TECHNOLOGIES AND THEIR POTENTIAL

We continue with the exploration of the forefront of AI advancements, highlighting technologies poised to reshape industries, society, and daily life. We talk about breakthroughs in quantum computing, enhancing AI's problem-solving capabilities, advancements in natural language processing that enable more nuanced human-computer interactions, and the integration of AI in biotechnology for groundbreaking healthcare solutions. These technologies, with their vast potential, underscore the urgency of ethical considerations and the need for collaborative innovation to ensure they benefit humanity as a whole, paving the way for a future where AI's possibilities are fully realized in harmony with human values.

It not only forecasts the acceleration of AI-driven innovation but also emphasizes the importance of steering these advancements toward societal well-being. The exploration of these technologies invites a proactive dialogue about the ethical implications of AI, advocating for a future where technology amplifies human potential, addresses global challenges, and operates within frameworks that prioritize equity, sustainability, and the collective good. This forward-looking perspective sets the stage for a future where AI and humanity co-evolve, unlocking new horizons of possibility and promise.

By examining innovations like AI avatars, digital twins, and quantum computing, emphasizing their ability to reshape interactions and enhance productivity. It highlights the significance of adopting these technologies responsibly, with a focus on privacy, security, and creating inclusive experiences. By understanding and leveraging these emerging technologies, businesses can navigate the challenges and opportunities they present, ensuring a future where technology and humanity coexist harmoniously.

- **Generative AI (GenAI)**: Revolutionizes content creation, design, and decision-making processes by learning from vast datasets.
- **Digital Twins**: Offer real-time simulations of physical objects or systems, enhancing predictive maintenance, and product development.
- **AI Avatars and Multimodal Interfaces**: Enhance user interactions through personalized and immersive experiences.
- **Quantum Computing**: Has the potential to solve complex problems exponentially faster than classical computers, impacting cryptography, material science, and optimization problems.
- **Blockchain and Web3 Technologies**: Provide decentralized, secure frameworks for transactions and interactions, complementing AI in ensuring data integrity and trust.

These technologies, among others highlighted by expert analyses like Gartner's, represent the forefront of AI integration, promising to redefine industries and societal norms. Each carries the potential to amplify AI's benefits, provided they are developed and deployed with ethical considerations and human-centric principles.

Based on the Gartner Emerging Technologies and Trends Impact Radar for 2024, the integration of AI with emerging technologies such as GenAI, digital twins, AI avatars, and quantum computing is highlighted. These technologies, each representing a pillar within the themes of smart world, productivity revolution, privacy and transparency, and critical enablers, are poised to significantly influence business strategies and societal interactions. Their potential for innovation spans enhancing online and offline convergence, revolutionizing productivity through AI advancements, strengthening data privacy, and enabling new applications through foundational tech developments. This integration underscores the necessity of ethical considerations and strategic planning to harness these technologies' transformative power effectively.

# SILICON EMPATHY: A VISION FOR THE FUTURE

"Silicon Empathy: A Vision for the Future" encapsulates the aspiration to seamlessly integrate AI with human empathy, fostering technologies that not only innovate but also care. This vision advocates for AI systems designed with an intrinsic understanding of human emotions, needs, and ethical considerations, ensuring technology enhances the human experience responsibly and inclusively. It envisions a future where AI and humans collaborate, leveraging the strengths of each to address societal challenges, improve quality of life, and create a more empathetic digital world.

The focus is on creating a symbiotic relationship between AI and human empathy, ensuring technologies are developed with a deep understanding of human values. This future envisions AI that not only solves complex problems but does so with a consideration for human emotions and ethical implications, embodying a partnership that leverages the best of technology and humanity to create a more understanding, equitable, and empathetically driven world.

We envision a world where AI technologies are inherently designed with empathy, understanding, and respect for human emotions and ethical standards. This future is characterized by AI systems that not only enhance efficiency and solve complex problems but also support and enrich human lives through thoughtful and sensitive interactions. The goal is to develop AI that acts as a complement to human abilities, bridging gaps in understanding and fostering a deeper connection between technology and the people it serves. This vision champions a collaborative approach, where technologists, ethicists, and users co-create AI solutions that prioritize well-being, inclusivity, and the common good, setting a new standard for how technology interacts with and impacts society.

In my envisioned future, AI serves as the intellectual powerhouse, akin to the "brain," guiding and enhancing our decision-making processes. Intelligent automation becomes the "hands," executing tasks with precision, thereby extending our capabilities into realms beyond our physical limits. At the center of this technological evolution, humans stand as the "heart," imbuing the entire system with empathy, ethical judgment, and creative thought. This triad of brain, hands, and heart fosters a future where technology amplifies human potential without supplanting our roles, reminiscent of how calculators enhanced mathematical capabilities without rendering the discipline obsolete. It's a future that sees technology as a tool for empowerment, mirroring historical transitions in agriculture and automation, where innovations lifted burdens rather than replacing human endeavor.

Reflecting on the agricultural evolution, the introduction of machinery and motors offered a profound example of technological advancement enhancing human productivity. Just as these innovations relieved horses of heavy labor, transforming agricultural practices, AI and intelligent automation promise to similarly revolutionize modern work. They are set to shoulder burdensome tasks, allowing humans to focus on areas where emotional intelligence and creativity are paramount, thus creating a future where technology and humanity advance in concert, each complementing the strengths of the other.

# THE ROAD AHEAD

As I embark on drafting "The Road Ahead", I approach it with a blend of anticipation and realism, guided by the understanding that the future, though uncertain, is ripe with potential. The journey of integrating AI into the fabric of our lives presents a dual pathway of challenges and opportunities. It's a future where the balance between human wisdom and technological advancement must be carefully navigated. The challenges, from ethical dilemmas to societal impacts, demand our vigilant attention and thoughtful action. Yet, the opportunities for growth, innovation, and enhancing human well-being are unparalleled. Embracing these possibilities requires a commitment to ethical development, collaborative innovation, and an openness to adapt as "time will tell" how this intricate dance between humanity and AI unfolds. This perspective encourages a hopeful yet cautious approach to the road ahead, emphasizing the potential for positive change while acknowledging the complexities that lie in navigating the unknown.

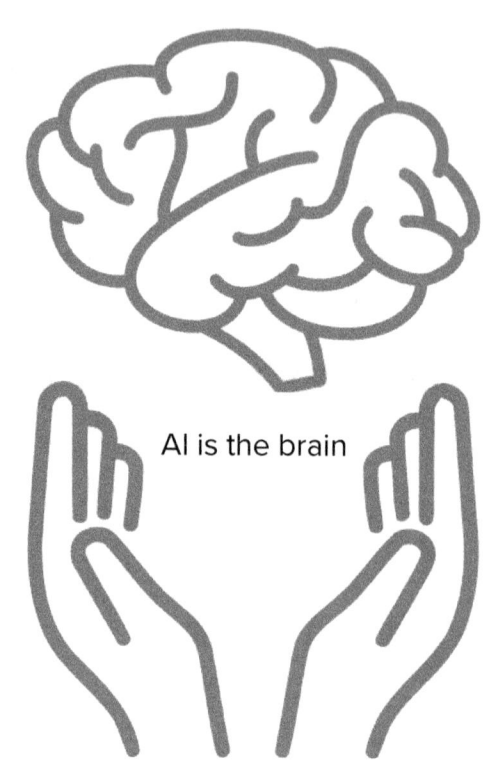

AI is the brain

Intelligent Automation are the hands

Humans are the heart

Working with your heart becomes a premium service

# EPILOGUE

Dear Reader,

We've reached the end of a journey together, one that has taken us through the intricacies and wonders of artificial intelligence, viewed through the lens of Silicon Empathy. As I reflect on the chapters we've traversed, from the dawn of AI to the dynamic present where AI blends seamlessly with human insight, my hope is that you've found both enlightenment and inspiration within these pages.

When I first presented the concept of Silicon Empathy, it was with the intent to spark a conversation about a future where AI serves not just our practical needs but also resonates with our emotional ones. This book has been an extension of that conversation, exploring how AI can be a tool for good, a means of amplifying our human capabilities rather than a replacement.

We've explored the power of AI to revolutionize industries, to bring efficiency to our work, and creativity to our passions. We've seen how it can transform customer experiences, making every interaction more personalized and impactful. Together, we've imagined a world where AI is not a cold, distant technology but one that is imbued with the warmth of human empathy.

Yet, with these possibilities, we've also considered the responsibilities. We've discussed the ethical dimensions of AI, the need for transparency, inclusivity, and the critical importance of keeping the human element central in the ever-evolving tapestry of technology.

As this book closes, my message is one of cautious optimism. The road ahead is filled with both challenges and opportunities. Time will indeed reveal the full impact of AI on our society, but with the guiding principles of Silicon Empathy, I am confident we can steer this technology toward a future that not only thinks but also feels.

Thank you for joining me on this journey. May the dialogue continue beyond these pages, as we collectively shape the role of AI in our lives with foresight, humanity, and empathy at the forefront.

*With Silicon Empathy,*
*Petrică Vlad*

# MY GIFT TO YOU ARE THE 10 COMMANDMENTS OF AI...

1. Prioritize Empathy: Design AI with an understanding of human emotions and needs.

2. Ensure Ethical Integrity: Embed ethical considerations into AI development from the start.

3. Promote Transparency: Make AI's decision-making processes clear and understandable.

4. Foster Inclusivity: Ensure AI technologies are accessible and beneficial to all.

5. Encourage Human Oversight: Maintain human involvement in AI decision-making to guide ethical and empathetic outcomes.

6. Champion Privacy: Protect user data and uphold stringent privacy standards.

7. Embrace Accountability: Be responsible for AI's impact and address any negative outcomes.

8. Support Collaboration: Work across disciplines to integrate diverse perspectives into AI development

9. Drive Positive Change: Use AI to address global challenges and improve human well-being.

10. Cultivate Continuous Learning: Adapt and evolve AI systems in response to changing societal values and technological advancements.

# ACKNOWLEDGEMENTS

This book would have never been possible if not for the many people that touched my life in a way or another. I want to mention my brother, Iuli, my parents, Cristina and Marian, my close family including my grandparents (some who passed and some who are still with us) and my godparents, the man whose name I proudly wear, Petrică *Eros* Ene, and Georgiana, and their family, Andrei and Andreea Mirică.

This wouldn't have happened without my friends and mentors that influenced my entire career, starting with Marian Sirghe, my first supervisor, Ioana Topală, who I will never forget for taking the risk of promoting a 19 year old in a lower management role, Nancy Montemayor, who managed to teach me that a good mentor can also be someone overseas, Cristi Alecu, the Harvey Specter to my Mike Ross, Horia Irimie, who gave me confidence to pursue my passion of working with data, Vasilis Delis, the executive whose door was always open, who always had time for me and who awoke in me the passion to speak in front of a public, Garima Gupta for having trust that I could handle a regional role, Paul Joustra who always pushed me to go further, and Felix Bradshaw, the man, the myth, the legend.

One man who I could never truly thank enough, who I feel like he treated me as his own son, and spent countless hours making me better, and hand-holding me through the world of Artificial Intelligence, Danny Kuivenhoven.

Saving for last the people who reminded me there is life after work, even though they had to put up with many cancellations and late arrivals due to long meetings and short deadlines, my bestfriends Adrian Briciu and Iulian Negrilă. Finally, to Alina Tkachenko, steadfast and inspiring, your impact is cherished.

To all, thank you!

# TABLE OF CONTENTS

About the Author   5

Structure   7

Prologue   9

The Genesis of Silicon Empathy   13

The Dawn of Artificial Intelligence   13

From Mechanical Brains to Emotional Beings   17

The Inspiration Behind Silicon Empathy   19

Understanding AI   22

The Basics of AI: What it is and isn't   22

Different Flavors of AI: NLP, Foundational & Generative   29

How AI Is Changing the World   39

The Human Connection   47

The Essence of Empathy in Technology   47

Stories of Technology Touching Lives   50

The Gap AI Can't Fill… Yet   54

Silicon Empathy in Action   55

Case Studies from Industry Giants   58

Small Businesses and Startups: A New Frontier   60

The Role of AI in Enhancing Customer Experience   64

| | |
|---|---|
| The Ethical Dimensions of AI | 67 |
| Navigating the Moral Maze | 67 |
| Privacy, Security, and Trust in an AI-Driven World | 70 |
| The Responsibility of Creators | 74 |
| Building a Bridge between AI and Humanity | 78 |
| Designing with Empathy: Principles and Practices | 78 |
| Encouraging Emotional Intelligence in AI Development | 82 |
| The Importance of Keeping Humans in the Loop | 84 |
| The Future Is Now | 89 |
| Emerging Technologies and Their Potential | 89 |
| Silicon Empathy: A Vision for the Future | 91 |
| The Road Ahead | 93 |
| Epilogue | 95 |
| Table of contents | 99 |

www.ingramcontent.com/pod-product-compliance
Lightning Source LLC
Chambersburg PA
CBHW071215240526
45470CB00018B/1871